WHO WAS THAT LADY?

CRAIG RICE: THE QUEEN OF SCREWBALL MYSTERY

Other books by Jeffrey Marks

Canine Crimes
Canine Christmas
Magnolias and Mayhem
The Ambush of My Name (A Ulysses Grant Mystery)

Coming soon:
Criminal Appetites

WHO WAS THAT LADY?

CRAIG RICE: THE QUEEN OF SCREWBALL MYSTERY

BY JEFFREY A. MARKS

DELPHI BOOKS
LEE'S SUMMIT, MISSOURI

ISBN: 0-9663397-1-1

Library of Congress Catalog Number: 00-191858

First Delphi Books printing April 2001

Manufactured in the United States of America

10 9 8 7 6 5 4 3 2 1

Cover design: Christina Albin Luboski

Book design: Donald R. Heyl

Quantity discounts are available on bulk purchases of this book.
For information contact:
DELPHI BOOKS
P.O. Box 6435
Lee's Summit, MO 64064
DELPHI BKS@AOL.COM

To Ellen Nehr who was an unending
source of inspiration and help, her knowledge
of mystery was and will always be unsurpassed
and "to Craig Rice, without whom this book
would not be possible"
(*Crime on My Hands* - George Sanders)

Acknowledgements

The amount of help I have received in writing this book has been legion. If I have left out a name, it is not from a lack of appreciation; it's only my faulty memory. For this many people to still care about a writer forty years after her death speaks volumes about her work and the people who make up the mystery community today.

I have found that this project has been a journey from its inception to completed book. During its time, this adventure has taken me from Venice Beach to Venice, Italy. Through research, I've touched some of the great lives of the twentieth century through Craig: Picasso; Auden; Gypsy Rose Lee; and Jack Kerouac. My friends, Deborah Adams and Sharyn McCrumb provided the impetus for the project as the origins of this book were discussed one night at a bar (I feel that Craig would approve) in Frankfort, Kentucky. As a result of their brainstorms, I was put in touch with Margaret Maron who has been an invaluable help to me in all phases of the project as well as writing the forward for this book. She in turn led me to Ellen Nehr who gave me more suggestions than I could follow up on in my own lifetime! Ellen walked along with me on this project and needs to be thanked immensely.

I have had contact with some of the best and brightest in the mystery field, from years past as well as today's practitioners. Barb D'Amato, Betty Nicholas, Jennifer Venola (Mrs. Stuart Palmer), Barry Zeman, Harold Masur, Dorothy B Hughes, Margaret Millar, John Dunning, Joan Hovey, Douglas Greene, Bill Pronzini, and Walter Albert have all dedicated some effort to answering my questions and guiding me in the right direction.

Not only writers, but editors as well have assisted me in bringing off this project. Sara Ann Freed of Mysterious Press sent me all the notes on Craig from the *Time* magazine morgue. Her generosity of time and patience is appreciated. Kate Stine has been so much help and encouragement, including buying the first chapter of this book for *The Armchair Detective*.

My research assistant, Eileen Callahan, has saved me hours of time by researching Craig's life in Chicago and the columns of her mystery review. Money wasn't enough for her to brave thirty below to find another set of reviews, but there was little else she didn't do with enthusiasm to help learn about Craig.

Erik Preminger has bent over backwards to help me with his generous effort of time and energy. He listened patiently and discussed theories of who wrote his mother's books.

I appreciate the endless discussions of bipolar disorders and mental health (including my own) with my friend, Dr. Scott Becker. For help with the death certificate, Joni Goldwasser who never bothers to ask why I need to know something. And John Greilick for his help with the photography. Alison Foster Jones has helped with proofreading and indexing all the characters I've run across in my research. Of course, any errors are mine, but she narrowed the scope and breadth of them. Special thanks to Karen Ireland for her meticulous editing. Christina Alta Luboski did a wonderful job on the cover, and helped with the images in the book. Donald R. Heyl for formatting the book. No list of accomplices would be complete without a mention of Deni Deitz who put me in contact with my publisher and now friend, Fran Baker of Delphi Books.

My own family has been incredibly gracious about accepting Craig Rice into our family when she occupied so much of my thought. Other families might have thought me crazy for spending so much time locked in the past. Mine accepted my mania and helped to talk about it as I could. My parents have always loved and accepted me for who I am, for that I am eternally and perpetually grateful. My sister is a rock of support in designer clothes, and her two boys will talk for hours with me about ideas for more books and more book parties.

The one sad note to all of this was the death of some of the principals during the writing of this book. Ellen Nehr's wealth of knowledge cannot be replaced. Margaret Millar died shortly after the start of my project. Dorothy B. Hughes was a charming lady who remembered Craig and shared her recollections with me without trying to hide Craig's flaws. Her daughter, Suzy, has taken time to send clips to me and help with this biography.

Most of all I appreciate the time and efforts of the family of Craig Rice. They opened their homes and their lives to me. Craig's life was not one that brought cheerful recollections and I'm not sure that I could have been as generous as they've been in recounting these memories to a stranger who wanted the truth. I consider them all my extended family now. Through their requests, I've had access to Craig's files at various libraries and the literary agent for the estate, Larry Janifer. Damaris Day, a Rice cousin, sent me reams of Rician poetry and clips. Howard Metcalfe, Iris' husband, saved me hours of searching for documents with his wonderful genealogy of the Rice family. David Ferguson has been incredibly helpful in providing information to me. His children (Lauren especially) have helped with research and timelines, and questions about their grandmother. Nancy Atwill Lessner has talked with me for hours about the past. Her children (especially Constance for her discussions of film and being my sounding board for revisions and Joe for being the brave one to make contact with me first) have all been of great help and I appreciate all of them.

INTRODUCTION

"Successful murder still requires imagination."[1]

Just after the end of World War II, after years of battles and body-counts, a war weary *Time* magazine decided to interview a major American mystery author for a cover story to give the country a change of pace.

Although the mystery genre began in America with Edgar Allan Poe, Americans had come late into the whodunit. British writers such as Agatha Christie, Dorothy L. Sayers, and G.K. Chesterton had long dominated the field. Time had more trouble finding an American author to put on the cover. They didn't want a firestorm over the selection. They wanted patriotic - and safe. Dashiell Hammett, the American author of five mysteries and the creator of hardboiled Sam Spade and dashing Nick and Nora Charles, hadn't published a novel since 1934, a dozen years earlier. His leftist political leanings made him less than an attractive choice for the interview. Nor was Raymond Chandler, the writer behind Philip Marlowe, any better. By 1946, he had only published four books in the Marlowe series, but he was already getting a reputation for being difficult to deal with, hard drinking and hard talking. Not the type for a family magazine.

Eventually, by process of elimination the *Time* editors decided on a female publishing phenomenon of the 1940s, Craig Rice. Reportedly, Erle Stanley Gardner, the author of the Perry Mason series, was miffed. He'd been considered back in the 1930s for this honor, but had been passed over in this round of consideration.

On paper, Craig looked like the perfect cover copy: she was a young (37), attractive brunette who wrote the madcap murder mysteries that sold like black market nylons. The tongue-in-cheek adventures of Jake and Helene Justus and John J. Malone, the boozy Windy City lawyer who never lost a client, brought smiles to a nation fighting a war overseas. As a tabloid reporter covering Midwest murder trials, she had learned to meet deadlines and routinely turned out two or three novels a year, along with short stories and screenplays.

Even FDR professed being a fan of Craig's. Her popularity was increasing due to film treatments of her work. A recent novel, *Home Sweet Homicide*, was being filmed (western hero Randolph Scott would star as Lieutenant Bill Smith). The novel was semi-autobiographical; an unorthodox mystery featuring a struggling crime writer's three children who solve a murder next door. Rice was a successful writer with three children.

Craig's popularity just after the war was at its peak. The magazine spoke with Pocket Books and discovered that the publishing firm gave small silver kangaroos as awards for selling a million copies in paperback. The first woman to receive the Gertrude (as the trademark kangaroo was called) would be either Craig Rice (whose *Trial By Fury* had sold over 550,000 copies at that point) or Agatha Christie.

The magazine chose Craig Rice for the cover story on January 28th, 1946. However, like the man who grabs the tiger's tail, the Time writers were unsure what to do with Craig once they had her. She wrote funny crime novels, but lived a less than humorous existence. The magazine staff were soon wondering if post-World War II America was ready for a much-married woman who drank, smoked and fought physical battles with her third husband, Larry Lipton.

The initial interview with Craig on March 21, 1945 should have fueled their doubts. She listed her first name as being Craig as well as her last name. She told that she had been born in a horse-drawn carriage, and that her father had been the Zamindar of Kagagooda.

None of these outlandish statements were true. All had been taken from the same imagination that had created her many mysteries. Who knows why she chose to lie to a national newsmagazine? Perhaps it was her demons or the desire to make herself more alluring or the fact that she had gotten away with such lies before or just plain perversity. But whatever the reasons, her lies were outrageous - and easily disproved.

For instance, Craig told the reporter that she had been born Catholic, implying that she had been raised in the faith. However, the family that raised her never took her to church and she was never baptized as a child. Only after daughter Nancy married a Catholic did Craig show any interest in the religion. In earlier interviews, Craig had expressed doubt in the existence of God and shocked people by boasting about having been married by a priest, rabbi, minister and a justice of the peace.

While that particular story held water, Craig went on to tell how: she married someone because she lost a coin toss; she forgot the name of the groom in that three day marriage; and she was the great-niece of Thomas Jefferson and a cousin of Winston Churchill.

However, the editors were impressed with Craig and her upcoming magazine, *Craig Rice Crime Digest*, being published by Anson Bond Publishing. The magazine was planned as a monthly, featuring summary-type reprints of mystery novels in the digest-sized magazine. Craig selected the novels and wrote true crime commentary for the magazine.

It wasn't until eight days before the publication of the cover story that the reporters were able to file a report with Craig's mother, Mary Randolph. Mary wasted no time in setting the reporters straight about Craig — or George (short for Georgiana) as Mary called her. She gave birth to her daughter in a Chicago hospital and denied all of Craig's claims to famous relatives including Winston Churchill and Thomas Jefferson. (The Randolphs, Mary's family were actually distant cousins of Thomas Jefferson although Craig insisted he was a great-uncle.) Her daughter had been named simply Georgiana Craig, although never christened in any church. Grimly, the *Time* reporters set to work trying to find the truth.

But just who was that lady? Excepting the *Time* article with its questionable veracity, facts are hard to come by about Craig Rice. While many biographies and critical works have been written about Christie (the woman who eventually beat Craig for the Gertrude), little is known about the woman who went by a man's name. Even in the twentieth-century with its information overload, she seems to have slipped under the radar. Her given name continues to vary with each mention. Her marriages and divorces are in dispute. Reviewers put them anywhere from three to eight husbands with an equal number of splits. Even the number of children she bore has been disputed. How could an author featured on the cover of America's premiere news-magazine be so mysterious about her personal life?

The confusion that was her personal life spilled over into her career as well. Contracts were lost or thrown away. Books were not promoted. Collaborative efforts were not followed up on. Her uncollected short stories sales went unreported. No wonder that her books today are limited to an occasional reprint of the Malone-Justus series. Her non-series novels, while included some of her best work, are only available from used bookstores.

Even so, she is still remembered fondly by the people who knew her, the reviewers, authors, and fans. She still stands alone at the top of the humorous mystery heap as the model of how funny murder can be.

CHAPTER O N E

"Her publisher swears that she was born in a horse-drawn carriage at the corner of Chicago's Michigan Avenue and 12th Street. . ."

If all unhappy families are unhappy in their own fashion, then the lack of parental role models in Georgiana Craig's family set them apart. To understand Georgiana's demons (and canon), one must understand her family as well. The impact is obvious. While the debate of nature vs. nurture in the development of personality continues, young Georgiana's family history most definitely played a part in her later writing.

Georgiana's mother, Mary Walker Randolph, had been born into a doctor's family in 1882. Her own mother, Mary Aglae Keen Randolph, died of typhoid just a month after the birth of her second child (also named Mary). Doctor and Mrs. Robert Innes Randolph lived in Manhattan, where Randolph had a successful medical practice as a general practitioner. Upon his wife's death, he sent his daughters to live with his mother-in-law, Mary Morris Walker, in Chicago. Randoph's own poor health prevented him from raising the children without assistance.

Randolph, born in 1852 in Washington, D.C., was descended from the Virginia Randolphs (from which Thomas Jefferson hailed). Fifty years after his death, Georgiana's mother still fondly remembered stories that her father had told about his efforts for the South in the Civil War, alongside three of his four brothers. Randolph's part in the war could have only been minimal due to his young age, but the family maintained a sense of history through the stories.

Their grandmother, yet another Mary, had considerable financial means, and raised Mary Randolph and her older sister, Ethel. Dr. Randolph moved his practice to Chicago after a period of time, and continued to treat patients there until 1889, when at the age of thirty-seven he died of a heart attack. Mary Randolph was only seven at the time of his death. By all accounts, Mary never missed her parents or showed emotion regarding their early passing. She took well to being raised by her grandmother.

The woman who would give birth to one of the funniest crime novelists of the twentieth century considered herself a serious artist. At the tender age of sixteen, Mary Randolph enrolled in the Art Institute of Chicago. The Art Institute (which resides with the Chicago Art Museum) offered a single course of study while allowing for areas of artistic concentration, ensuring that each student became well versed in all areas of the arts.

While studying sculpting at the institute, Randolph met another young artist, Harry Moshiem Craig. Throughout 1897 and 1898, the pair studied the classical arts curriculum of the school. Craig (whom Randolph nicknamed Bosco for an unknown reason) was studying to be a painter. With his dark curly hair and boyish face, Craig appeared the likable rogue who didn't take life too seriously. Randolph was striking even as a young woman, with beautiful cheekbones and a slender, striking figure. She became a favorite subject of Craig's. The pair hit it off immediately, and were known to court off the Institute's campus.

In the fall of 1899, Craig dropped out of the Institute, most likely for lack of funds. His departure turned Randoph's romantic attention in other directions. A few months later, at the age of eighteen Mary married Joseph Davoll. Little is known of Randolph's first husband beyond his name. The marriage was not a success and ended in divorce in less than a year, a shocking occurrence at the turn of the century in polite society. It is known that Randolph left school to become the dutiful housewife, which most likely didn't sit well with the well-to-do artist. The couple didn't remain in contact after the split. Randolph was not the kind of woman who looked back after making decisions. She rarely spoke of him again.

Randolph soon re-enrolled in the Art Institute, having missed the artistic outlet and the association with people of similar interests. The domestic demands of nineteenth century matrimony were not for her. Randolph found a second home at the Institute when she returned. She also resumed seeing Bosco Craig.

In 1906, Randolph and Craig married. Mary Craig inherited a substantial sum from the wealthy grandmother who had raised her, and so the Craigs decided to travel Europe to practice their respective arts. Young, in love, and well-to-do-what better combination for open-ended travel? They made no plans to return to the States when they took off. The Craigs' itinerary included the great art capitals of Europe, including London, Paris and Munich.

Van Gogh, Gauguin, and Cezanne all lived in Paris, and the pull of the artistic capital drew in the Craigs. The art world had changed dramatically in the decade before the Craigs' descent on Europe. Picasso left behind the work of his "Blue Period" to start painting what would later be called Cubism. Chagall and others transformed the art world, heralding the age of modern art. Europe offered more than could be hoped for in the Midwest, even Chicago.

Mary Craig basked in the creative genius of Europe. Living amongst these artists encouraged her to strive to better her work and be more critical of her own attempts. She was very productive in Europe, though she often destroyed a work that she didn't like. Working with clay and granite made her relatively stationary, as it was nearly impossible to lug the oversized art around the world. Bosco Craig's painting supplies were much more mobile. Hence, Mary Craig trashed many of the less-than-stellar works for ease of travel.

After two years of studying art in Europe, Mary Craig found herself pregnant, and returned to Chicago in early 1908 to have her first child. She traveled alone. Bosco Craig remained in Europe, painting and enjoying life. He trusted that the independent Mrs. Craig would be fine on a long ship journey home while pregnant. Though no correspondence exists between the couple, solitary travel was not a good sign for the relationship. The serious Mary Craig and carefree Bosco Craig were not well suited for living together. Mary Craig hadn't yet forsaken her family duties, though. She divided her time between her sister and Craig's mother in Fort Atkinson, Wisconsin.

Georgiana Craig was born on June 5, 1908, at St. Luke's Hospital in Chicago. Contrary to her daughter's publicist's later stories of birth in a horse-drawn carriage and a mother unwilling to leave the Art Institute, Mary Craig made it to the hospital for the birth of her daughter. Hospitals were still a luxury for childbirth at the turn of the century, but Craig expected and received the very best in medical care. Georgiana Craig's story only underscores the rift between the generations, and the hard feelings over Mary Craig having put her career before her first-born child.

Wanting to rejoin her new husband in Europe as soon as possible, Mary Craig returned to the continent as soon as she medically could. Alone. She left the baby with Bosco Craig's mother, Mary Church Young Craig, in Fort Atkinson. A baby would slow her progress and interfere with the couple's travel and pursuit of the arts. Having no parents of her own, the new mother seemed unconcerned about the maternal role in childrearing. After all, she had been raised by a grandmother and had turned out fine. Although she had been raised in a household of women, Mary Craig had wanted a boy, a male heir. The reasons for this are not clear, but interviews with her make the preference for men apparent. Her quick departure from Chicago underscored this disappointment in little Georgiana's gender.

Like many traditional families of the day, Bosco Craig's mother didn't live alone. Also living at her home in Fort Atkinson were Craig's half-sister and her husband, Nan and Elton Rice. Bosco Craig had been the only child of Mary Church Young Craig's second marriage (to Samuel Craig); however, her previous marriage to James Young had produced three daughters: Mary Eloise Young, known as Mame; Nancy Church Young, known as Nan; and Jessica Young, called Jesse. Although Bosco Craig's half-sisters were a generation older than he was, all three remained close to home and watched him as he grew up. The sisters spoiled their younger brother terribly, being more like aunts than sisters to little Bosco.

Nan and Elton Rice had been unable to conceive a child of their own, and started raising their half-niece as the daughter they couldn't have. In their forties, the pair had given up hope of having a child. The couple poured out their love on this pseudo-orphan, quickly spoiling her.

Nan Rice was a small, slight woman who had been called Chip by her father because of her diminutive stature. She and Elton Rice made an unusual couple for their day-extremely well-educated and independent-minded. Nan Rice had been a Montessori-type school-teacher long before women worked prior to marriage, and Elton Rice had retired from the white-collar world of banking.

In addition, Nan Rice was an ardent feminist, teaching Georgiana that she could be anything a man could be. Mrs. Rice marched as a suffragette and followed politics closely. The couple were also devout Democrats, who kept a picture of FDR enshrined in the living room during the 1930s. They didn't participate in organized religion, which made them even more unique in the small town of Fort Atkinson. As a result, Georgiana was never baptized or christened after her birth. Quite an unusual set of circumstances for the first years of the century.

Despite some difficulties in caring for a newborn without the birth mother, Nan and Elton Rice adapted well to the situation. Mary and Bosco Craig would not visit Georgiana until she turned three. When the Craigs returned to the U.S. in 1911, they reclaimed their daughter on a quick trip to Fort Atkinson and moved to Chicago, where they continued to pursue their interests in painting and sculpture. Mary Craig enrolled once more at the Art Institute, to apply some of the techniques she had learned in Europe.

While legally the birth parents could take their child wherever they chose, uprooting the three-year old from the only home she knew had a tremendous psychological impact on Georgiana. The loss of security and sense of home traumatized her in an emotional upheaval akin to losing one's parents. Even as an adult, she would mention the abandonment, and it was the major theme in her fiction. She didn't take well to the new family situation or to Chicago. Nan and Elton Rice were heart-broken over the loss of the child they now considered their own.

Despite this domestic instability, Georgiana remained a precocious child and learned to read by the age of four. The little girl questioned everything, and possessed a vivid imagination. She was a bookish child, hampered by a number of allergies and illnesses. Photos taken at the tine show a thin and gangly Georgiana with thick dark hair like her father, and chubby cheeks that dimpled when she smiled.

Living in Chicago didn't suit Georgiana's parents, either. After three years in the United States, they decided to return to Europe to paint and sculpt-again without their daughter. They left Georgiana with the Rices for a second time. They assumed that the couple would be willing to take the child back on the same terms as before: raise her until we want her back. By age six, in effect, Georgiana had been orphaned three times, and in the process left with absolutely no sense of belonging or family. She clung to Nan and Elton Rice when she returned to them, afraid of losing them again. Despite an inquisitive nature that presumed a certain independence, Georgiana was extremely needy emotionally, and demanded a great deal of attention from the Rices. As an only child, she was able to receive most of the family's focus.

Nan and Elton Rice were happy to take back Georgiana. Shortly after, the Rices left retirement for a more bucolic existence. They moved to Washington state (near the Canadian border) to run a commercial apple orchard. Records do not make clear whether the Rices owned or merely tenanted the farm, but they were responsible for the crop of apples grown there. The couple dabbled in horticultural science as they farmed.

The farm life agreed with Georgiana; she was a sickly child who needed a great deal of medical attention. She had contracted a number of respiratory infections. The girl had suffered from a number of allergies to foods including strawberries, which made her break out in hives. The quiet atmosphere of the orchard allowed Georgiana to grow and be nurtured by the Rices without outside influences.

Mary and Bosco Craig's timing for leaving America couldn't have been worse. They arrived in Europe in early 1914. Secret alliances conceived by the heads of state in Europe, and the assassination of the Archduke Ferdinand, began a chain of events that led to the outbreak of fighting in the Balkans, quickly engulfing the continent. When war broke out in Europe in August, 1914, the Craigs hurriedly decided to move to Bombay, India. They had spent just a few months on the continent that had afforded them so much pleasure before the start of World War I and a forever-changed Europe. In Asia, they continued their artistic pursuits, but the challenge of their life, along with the lack of artistic outlets, took a toll on the couple.

In 1918, Mary Craig returned to the United States when she became pregnant for a second time. A deadly flu epidemic had swept the Far East, killing millions of people globally. Craig wanted to be far away from possible infection when she gave birth. By this time, traveling with Bosco Craig had lost its appeal, and she started making plans to remain in the United States after the birth of her second child.

Bosco Craig decided to stay in the Far East, and continued to travel extensively in the Orient. Without his wife's money, the charming rogue had to make a living on his own. In order to support the lifestyle Mary Craig had provided, he gave up his painting career to become a land broker. He had never been very serious about his art. Mary Craig considered herself a sculptress above all else, including mother. Later in life, she reflected that Bosco Craig could have been a good painter if he had bothered to apply himself, but no one can really verify that assumption. The only known remaining work by Craig is a striking portrait of his wife, presently held by Craig's son-in-law, Howard Metcalfe.

Mary and Bosco Craig's son, Christopher, was born in February of 1919. Without seeing each other again, the Craigs divorced soon after. By this time, Georgiana was almost eleven and had little memory of her birth parents. Her life was with the Rices, who took care of her scraped knees and colds. However, on her way to live in Santa Fe, Mary Craig stopped in Washington to retrieve her daughter. With the birth of her second child, the long-awaited son, Craig had decided to settle down and raise both children by herself. Whatever reception she was expecting, it certainly wasn't the outburst that young Georgiana provided.

"Go to hell," she told her mother. While few stories of Georgiana Craig's youth remain, the family was clear that she adamantly refused to move again.

Georgiana's decision to stay was the opening salvo in what would be a lifelong battle between mother and daughter, played out over decades, across continents, and in the news media.

Georgiana had been raised to think independently, and the child harbored extreme bitterness over being left by her birth parents. Raising her voice and cursing, she expressed her determination to live with the Rices. With the exception of the few years in Chicago, Nan and Elton Rice had raised Georgiana from a few days old. She gave her undivided love to these people, not the Craigs. Mary Craig left the farm with only baby Christopher. Scorned, she took her daughter's words seriously and didn't maintain maternal relations with the girl after that fight. Even in later years, she barely acknowledged the fact that she'd had a first-born daughter.

Mary Craig didn't forgive Georgiana for choosing to remain with her half-aunt and uncle, and took a malicious pleasure in spurning her in public at every opportunity. Georgiana, however, tried to forge a relationship with Craig despite wanting to remain with the Rices. She referred to Nan and Elton Rice as her foster-parents, and still called Mary "Mother." Craig, in return, rejected her daughter when she could, to punish her for choosing the Rices over her. On one occasion, she embarrassed Georgiana by turning away from a kiss in others' company. Mary Craig was also known for only speaking about her sons, and not "that girl" as she referred to Georgiana. Even when she was interviewed for *Time* in 1946, Craig was still hostile about the rejection, referring to her daughter as "George,"[1] and saying that she didn't have time to read her daughter's books.

After this episode with Mary Craig, Nan and Elton Rice formalized their relationship with Georgiana by adopting her in 1921. Mary signed the paperwork approving the adoption, and the girl was now officially named Georgiana Craig Rice, called Anna by her adoptive parents. One more name for the child. They continued to live on the small farm, in the Okanogan Valley in Washington State, only a few miles south of the Canadian border. Nan Rice taught herself to graft the apple trees, and experimented with the orchard while raising Anna. The family enjoyed a quiet, bucolic existence. The small town didn't offer a lot in the way of social activities, and kept the family close to home where they could concentrate on Georgiana's education and her emotional needs. Without the distractions, Georgiana was able to grasp a number of subjects and receive the attention and love she needed.

Living in Washington, Georgiana was taught mainly by private tutors who emphasized history, music, and languages. Her sharp intelligence and artistic nature began to show. By the time she reached twelve, Georgiana had a rough knowledge of Latin and Greek. There seemed to be no end to her range of interests or her ability to pick up a subject quickly if she was interested.

Attempts at a more formal education didn't work as well. Georgiana's neediness and desire to cling to Nan and Elton Rice made separation nearly impossible. She wanted to stay at home at all costs. On several occasions, when Georgiana was sent to a boarding school, she ran away or behaved so badly that she was returned home-the end result she desired. Georgiana Rice couldn't stand to be away from her loved ones, not even for short periods of time. Until almost the end of her life, Nan Rice would be a constant companion to Georgiana.

She was happiest as a child in the company of Nan and Elton Rice, and while creating. Georgiana began writing poetry when she was nine years old. When she was only ten, one of her poems won a contest for a Chicago newspaper. Even these poems show a twinkle of the humor and wit that she would use in later years-a play on words, an image to make the reader smile.

It's very hard to think of
The way men do these days;
The way they try to kill each other
In ten thousand different ways.
I don't think God intended
That His children all should fight
And have to keep sentries on guard

Whether its [sic] day or night.
The kaiser wants to rule the world
I think he is a pig;
Or else he's made of sausages,
And they are awfully big.

Nan and Elton Rice exhibited no gifts for the creative arts, but they encouraged their daughter at every opportunity, trying to mold her artistic nature. Georgiana wrote dozens of poems that Nan Rice lovingly bound into small books with pictures to accompany the verse. Georgiana also studied piano, and in those early years hoped to train as a concert pianist. The Rices helped by providing her with lessons and sheet music.

Georgiana's real mother continued to pursue her own creative arts. When she left Georgiana with the Rices, Mary Craig moved to the Chama Valley (about one hundred miles from Santa Fe). She soon met an artist in New Mexico who went by the name Sacha Finklestein. With his penchant for stories and confusing names, the man could have easily posed as Georgiana's father. A Russian by birth, Alexander Illytch Patraeff, he was said to have been in turn a count and a prince in Bessarabia; however, the number of Finklesteins in the royal court was slim. More likely the ethnic surname marked him as being of Jewish heritage, and thus targeted for a pogrom. Many Russian refugees claimed a noble heritage, since the Communists had destroyed any records that might refute such a claim. An aura of mystery surrounded these outcast royals. Finklestein left the country at the onset of the Bolshevik Revolution in 1919 and moved to Paris, where he studied art. Many of the so-called White Russians, the elite of the czarist society, fled the country at this time and sought shelter elsewhere. After a short stay in Western Europe, Finklestein immigrated to the United States.

Finklestein arrived in Santa Fe at the same time as Mary Craig. Like Bosco Craig, he painted and exhibited his work, under the name of F.I. Sacha. Mary Craig enjoyed the time at the artists' community in New Mexico, as she put on two exhibitions of her own sculptures. She felt fulfilled in the company of others artists, as she had been at the Institute and in Europe. Again, she began courting an artist.

Finklestein and Mary Craig married in or about 1922. Because of his dislike of his own surname at that time, Finklestein adopted the surname Randolph, Mary's maiden name. Mary Walker Randolph Davoll Craig Finklestein became Mary Randolph once more. This name change and Georgiana's adoption added to the confusion regarding Georgiana's real name.

The stories surrounding her name became almost as convoluted as a Craig Rice plot. Critical works in later years would assume that Rice's maiden name was the same as her mother's married name; hence, almost all of the articles about the mystery writer would label her Georgiana Randolph or even Georgiana Walker Randolph. She found this confusion amusing and didn't bother to correct misunderstandings. Instead, she fueled them. Private jokes amused her most, especially when they resulted in public confusion. Later, Rice would add to the doubts by giving out variations of her real name, delighting in fooling people. By the 1980s the subject was so murky that researchers confidently stated that no indication remained of how the author had selected the pseudonym "Craig Rice." They labeled her penname a mystery. How ironic that in fact it was her full, adopted name.

Shortly after the Randolph's wedding, the couple and Christopher set off for Europe, traveling extensively around the continent. While living in Czechoslovakia in 1924, Mary Randolph gave birth to a third child, another son, named Alexander after his father. The growing family bought a home overlooking the Grand Canal in Venice, where Christopher and Alexander were raised.

Georgiana Rice had little contact with her birth family at this point. She didn't know of the birth of her second brother until much later in life. About the same time, the Rices sold the commercial orchard and decided to travel. Georgiana Rice had graduated from Oroville High School in May 1924, and soon the family migrated south to move in with Nan Rice's sister, Mame Young, in San Diego. Young was much older than her sister, and large compared to the diminutive Nan Rice. She had been a schoolteacher, and had moved to La Jolla many years prior. Her efforts on behalf of young Georgiana Rice were needed. Attempts to educate the Rices' daughter were proving futile. Georgiana had grown into a very headstrong young woman, bright and lively, charming and gay, but also incredibly stubborn. Nan and Elton Rice doted on her, not reproaching her behavior, which didn't help the situation.

While living with Mame Young, Georgiana Rice attended the State Teacher's College (later San Diego State University), majoring in letters and science. The Rices and Mame Young all encouraged Georgiana in her studies. By this time, she was showing traces of being the funny young woman remembered by her schoolmates as the class clown. She made more of an impression on the boys in her class with her glamorous looks. Georgiana was still the slender young woman with dark hair of earlier photos, but her cheeks had thinned out, leaving her with the beautiful bone structure of her mother. The attractive brunette wore her hair short to keep the curls under control. She was quite a beauty.

By the mid-1920s, Rice enjoyed the looser, less studious mentality of the flappers on campus, not bothering to spend time on her class work. The post-war years had allowed women a bit more freedom in their actions, along with the right to vote. As a result, Rice became a cut-up in class. Schoolrooms became a theater for her antics.

Rice only lasted a year at the school, mostly because of her failing grades. Not a surprise for a woman who was more interested in entertaining than matriculating. She had tasted the fruits of what her quick wit could get her-unlimited attention and laughter. Grades were secondary at that point. Ironically, Rice received her worst grades in the subjects directly relating to her natural parents: History of Modern Europe and Art Structure.

Although Georgiana Rice didn't fare well in her studies, she blossomed in her creative efforts. She tried any number of the arts before settling down to one. Unsure of her own talents and interests, Rice attempted several artistic endeavors before she discovered her passion for writing. Although she tickled the ivories informally at the parties she was learning to love, Rice had given up hope of becoming a concert pianist. She joined The State College Players at State Teacher's College and participated in the dramas there. At one point, she played the lead role in a performance for a local school, acting the part of beauty in *The Prince who Learned Everything out of Books*. Finally, Rice worked for a reform newspaper while she was in college, earning a salary of $6 a week. She found that she enjoyed the daily change of work brought on by the news and the excitement of unfolding events, re-creating the scenes for her readers. "I unwittingly uncovered the wrong scandal, got fired, took the scandalous information to a rival paper, got hired at twice the salary,"[2] she told Fred Dannay years later. By the time she left, Rice worked as a police reporter for the newspaper at the wage of $22.50. These days of crime, courts, and lawyers made a big impression on her, and she remembered them often in her letters and essays. She regaled friends with the story of this trial or another, using the court cases, which seemed to be burned into her mind as well as the court record. At this point, Rice gave up her aspiration of working on any other creative art, and applied herself solely to writing. After watching their daughter's disastrous freshman year at State Teacher's College, Nan and Elton Rice chose to return to Fort Atkinson. Georgiana Rice followed them to start her career as a journalist.

CHAPTER T W O

". . . an unknown, young woman was writing radio scripts, in Chicago."

In 1926, Nan and Elton Rice moved back to Fort Atkinson to live with Nan's mother, Mary Church Young Craig, the same woman who had taken in Georgiana Rice almost twenty years earlier. Still living in the same house at 607 South Main Street, Mrs. Craig was approaching ninety and in ill health. Nan and Elton Rice moved in to help with her care. Georgiana Rice came with them, unwilling to be left in California. Time would later refer to Rice's return to the Chicago area as "a decade of failure and booze.[1]" The description seems excessively harsh for a woman who started a family and learned the basics of her trade in those same ten years.

While the Rices cared for Mrs. Craig, Georgiana Rice moved to Chicago and started dating Arthur John Follows. Jack, as his friends knew him, was a thirty-four year old Englishman who had immigrated to this country in 1910. A soft-spoken, gentle man, he had served in the Canadian army during World War I and had seen fighting in France, Belgium, and Germany during the war. Gassed with chemical weapons during battle, he returned home with damaged lungs.

Upon his return to the United States, Follows decided to pursue his education. He completed a high school education at Washington High in Milwaukee, and later began college classes at Beloit University in Wisconsin. He, like Rice, wrote poetry and worked as a journalist. His parents had been artistic in nature, earning a living as itinerate actors. They died suddenly, in an accident, in the late 1890s.

There was a sixteen-year gap in the couple's ages (her 18 to his 34). Rice's attraction to older men during this period most likely stems from her not having had a relationship with her birth father. Her only meetings with her father occurred before she was in elementary school. What she did learn of Bosco Craig was through her half-aunts, who had doted on him as a boy. She'd grown up with an idealized image of the man.

Bosco Craig remained abroad, writing to family members on rare occasions. Georgiana Rice strongly resented the mother who popped in and out of her life, but her father had stayed in the Orient, never returning to the U.S. to visit his only daughter, or even to meet his son, Chris. Rice didn't seem to resent him as she did her mother. By dating someone nearly twice her age, she recaptured a part of her childhood that she had missed. Relatively sheltered as a child in a farm community, the only man in Rice's life had been Elton Rice, another much older man. The theme of the absent father turns up repeatedly in Rice's fiction, showing that this subject remained on her mind.

Rice toyed with the idea of going back to college in Chicago, and had her transcripts forwarded from the State Teacher's College in San Diego to Northwestern University in early in 1928. Not much would have transferred in the way of credits, as she'd failed most of her classes, but the paperwork was still required. However, she never began classes at the school on the northern edge of Chicago. Fate had other plans for her. Rice became pregnant with her first child. Jack Follows and Georgiana Craig Rice were married on October 28, 1927 in a small Episcopalian ceremony at St. Peter's Church in Chicago, and honeymooned in Fort Atkinson, staying with Nan and Elton Rice. Nancy Melville Follows was born on June 26, 1928. Most of the time,

Rice and Follows left Nancy with a hired nurse. Rice continued to write as much as she could, while Jack worked to support the young family.

Rice and Follows chose to live in Chicago, and their second child, Iris Patricia Follows, was born a year later, on June 25, 1929. The family bliss was short-lived. Just as Mary and Bosco Craig had returned to Europe on the eve of World War I, Iris was born on the cusp of the Great Depression. When the stock market tumbled, and people realized there was no chicken in every pot, Follows lost his newspaper job. He had difficulty finding another position in journalism. Rice's freelance assignments grew fewer, and the couple began to have money troubles. Rice had never been good at managing a family budget, content to live from hand to mouth, and being ambidextrous about it. Money went for fun rather than to cover the mounting bills. The nurse that had been watching the children went unpaid, and the Follows' put their children in an orphanage as an interim solution to some of the money problems. The couple couldn't stay in their home, and had to move out. While Jack Follows tried to scrape up the money to send the girls to England to live with his relatives, Nan and Elton Rice rescued the children and took them into their home in Fort Atkinson. The once childless couple began raising a second family from infancy.

The Follows' marriage disintegrated in the aftermath of losing the children and the income. Rice's marriage ended in divorce in 1931. One of the Follows' friends in Chicago was a man named Albert Ferguson. He and Jack Follows had been friends for several years, both journalists. Ferguson, several years older than Follows, served as a mentor figure of sorts to the young writer.

To Georgiana Rice, he was much more.

Rice had started seeing Ferguson in Chicago. He was a kindred spirit. He moved frequently: having been born in Washington, D.C., he lived in New York, and edited *TheRotarian* in Evanston, a suburb north of Chicago, as well as *The Young Republican* magazine in Chicago. Much older than Rice, Ferguson had been born the same year as her mother had. He was more established than his friend Jack Follows and was able to maintain a job during the harrowing years of the Depression. He and Rice developed a relationship that became more open following the divorce.

Having been repeatedly left by Mary and Bosco Craig, Rice had trouble forming permanent relationships, and staying focused on one thing. Nowhere did this become more evident than her marriages. She filled up her life with activities, so that if one part of her life went away, she wouldn't miss it. Rice had severe separation anxiety over the failure of any relationship. Even when she wanted a separation from a man, the angst over the split caused her to become depressed and moody. She felt a certain amount of stability in her relationship with her adopted family. In that environment, she felt free to be herself and express her feelings. The suppression of her innate personality caused a certain amount of trouble and resentment in Rice that tended to come out in inappropriate ways. With her classmates, she made them laugh to be liked. With suitors, she became a model of what they expected in a wife. With Jack Follows, she tried the role of loving wife and mother. While involved with Ferguson, she became a literate companion to the man.

While Rice was traveling with her new companion in 1932, Nan Rice's mother died. The old woman's home was bequeathed equally to her three daughters. Since the Rices lived in the home, they bought the two-thirds interest from Mame and Jesse Young, and for a second time began to raise a family. Although the Rices had enjoyed the orchard in Washington, they felt Fort Atkinson was home. They were now raising two more children. The couple had to take their welfare into consideration. They weren't sure if this arrangement would be temporary, or how the Depression would impact the situation. Nan and Elton Rice decided to make their move back to Wisconsin permanent.

Even after the divorce, Rice made no attempt to retrieve her children. She knew that the Rices would care for her children properly, and she was busy traveling and writing with Ferguson. Jack Follows left Chicago, brokenhearted at losing his young bride to a friend, broke, and unable to find work. He moved to Milwaukee, where he located a WPA writing job after working in the tool and die industry for several years. By the time he could scrape together enough money to provide for his children, he'd lost track of his family.

For reasons no one will ever understand, Rice repeated the familiar pattern of her own mother by abandoning her children. Despite the deep-seated resentment at being handed off to another couple and its impact on her, she also chose to leave her children. No one questioned

Rice's love for her children as frequently expressed in her letters and interviews, but she appeared happier to leave their daily rearing to someone else, so that she could devote herself to her husbands and writing. As her mother before her, Rice never seemed to realize the emotional impact of that choice on her or her children. Having been isolated as a child, she thought this was a normal situation.

The Depression and the purchase of the Ft. Atkinson home had taxed the retirement finances of the Rices. Settling into Fort Atkinson again, Elton Rice was elected the clerk of courts for Jefferson County shortly after the family's return to the area, and commuted the five miles to Jefferson, the county seat, on a regular basis. Additionally, the couple needed a more substantial income to support the girls as neither Follows nor Rice was helping them financially. Nan and Elton Rice soon returned to the quiet life they had known before they left for Washington with Georgiana. Nan Rice busied herself with a weekly group known as the Tuesday Club, and her gardening. As the Rices were now in their sixties, some concessions were made to the changes in the household. A daily was hired to take care of the children and do some of the cleaning for the couple. Along with general dusting and sweeping duties, the help woke the children and fed them breakfast.

Though Georgiana Rice's children lived with the elder Rices, Nancy found herself, at an early age, caring for Iris. Unlike Georgiana, an only child, the girls had each other. Without a mother, the sisters stayed close, sharing friends and activities. When Nancy went off to kindergarten, the school allowed Iris to attend even though she was a year younger, and technically ineligible.

Although Rice did not live with her adoptive parents at this time, she visited their home on occasion. Some of the people in Fort Atkinson were scandalized by the behavior of this attractive, flashy woman who smoked, and (by this time) was rumored to drink. While talked about in whispers, the writer was considered a glamorous figure in the small town. Only twenty-three, she had let her hair grow longer and wore the dark curls up on her head, giving her a gypsy look. Rice only drank on social occasions, but managed to have frequent parties and get-togethers with her friends in Chicago to mask her growing dependence on alcohol. The numerous parties on Rush Street in Chicago (known for its bars and clubs) had put a spell on her. Small town life was not ready for a divorced woman who had abandoned her children, and lived "in sin" with another man.

Rice had a hard time combining the Fort Atkinson expectations of Nan and Elton Rice with the hard-driving newspaper world in which she worked, where women were expected to drink and curse right along with the men. To succeed meant being as tough as the guys, yet women who engaged in these behaviors received whispers and dirty looks from the polite society of the Rice family. Rice looked down her nose at the matrons as she jumped into the world of journalism with both feet. She reveled (as she had earlier) in the world of news and events. She continued to love the crime beat, and tried to work it as much as possible. As her success grew, she justified her behavior to the Fort Atkinson residents, now thrilled about the writer in town. Still, in the first years following her divorce, returning to Wisconsin proved uncomfortable.

"Georgiana" was dropped at this point to use the by-line of Craig Rice for her writing. While she and Ferguson lived together, Rice continued to write to support herself. Women working in the good old boy network of journalism were practically unheard of during the early 1930s. Wanting to be accepted into the journalistic crowd, Rice used a masculine pseudonym, and frequently didn't acknowledge her gender in the text of an article. It was better to be assumed a man. Only when photographs of the dark-haired woman appeared with the narrative could the reader determine that Craig Rice was an attractive female reporter. Again, Rice delighted in fooling people into thinking she was a man, enjoying the confusion her name created.

Unlike the constant turmoil that Craig Rice seemed to thrive on, the family household of the elder Rices was peaceful, since Nan and Elton Rice rarely argued. Nan Rice insisted on a non-violent household and never spanked the children when they misbehaved. As Nan Rice had been a teacher, the couple used the same approaches to stimulate Georgiana Rice's daughters intellectually as they had with Rice when she was young, reading to the girls and stressing literature. Ralph Waldo Emerson was a particular favorite of Elton Rice's, and he read his works to the children frequently. Without the concerns of young Georgiana's separation anxiety issues, the Rices were able to send the girls to public school for the majority of their education.

In comparison to the quiet home of the Rices, Craig Rice seemed to have mastered juggling five balls at once. She was happiest when totally immersed in several projects at the same time. Rice's friends remember her as someone who could do more things at one instant than most could do in a day. She always managed to find time to write, attend the Rush Street parties, and travel with Ferguson. She needed several freelance assignments to make ends meet in those impoverished times. Among Rice's many jobs was her work as a copywriter at WCLO, the Janesville, Wisconsin, radio station where she wrote advertisements and news items. She also worked at *The Green Sheet Journal*, a newspaper, as a part-time writer.

In addition, she worked as the radio editor for the *Beacon Syndicate*, a Wisconsin magazine. In one of the few examples of her early work, Rice decried the number of bad scripts being produced for radio, and the need for higher standards. Part of her duties included radio criticism, a skill she would use later as a mystery critic.

Rice and Ferguson lived together on the north side of Chicago near Evanston, where Ferguson edited *The Rotarian* and traveled to New York on a regular basis. They were a part of the drinking crowd that frequented the Rush Street bars, patronized by the big names in Midwest entertainment and sports. Despite their long history together, no record can be found of a marriage between Georgiana Craig Rice and Albert Ferguson. The Rice family believes that Ferguson couldn't marry Craig because he was already married. His wife had suffered a mental illness and divorce was out of the question. However, that did not stop Rice from introducing Ferguson as her husband, and counting him in the totals of the men she married.

Not that Rice would have avoided another marriage at this point in her life. It would have been during this timeframe that the apocryphal wedding would have occurred in which she lost a coin toss, and married a man. She reported to *Time* that the marriage only lasted three days. However, a search of the Cook County records shows no license for Rice and the mystery gentleman. Since Rice remained reticent on the details of this wedding, the story was probably just another amusing anecdote told to entertain her friends. Craig Rice was not above telling a story to make people laugh. Sometimes, when she repeated it often enough, the story gained ground as being fact, rather than the charming exaggerations of a woman who wanted to make people laugh.

Long-time business friend and fellow mystery writer Dorothy B. Hughes recalled that Rice often told incredibly outlandish stories about herself, most of which were unbelievable to the listener, who later found out that there was a grain of truth in the tale. One such tale was her claim to be the great-grandniece of Thomas Jefferson. A distant relationship was there, but nothing quite as intimate as what she described. She claimed to be related to royalty, relying on her stepfather's claim to be of the Russian royal court.

While staying in New York with Ferguson on one of his frequent trips to the city, Rice had her third child and only son, David Craig Rice, later renamed David Elton Ferguson. Whatever the later outcome of their romance, she and Ferguson were not married at the time of David's birth. David is said to have discovered a copy of his birth certificate as a child, realizing that his parents hadn't been married. The change of his name from Rice to Ferguson at a later date lends credence to that theory. He was born on April 8th, 1932, in Manhattan.

As Rice and Ferguson continued to travel, their child was placed in a foster home at the age of three. Like Rice, David was a sickly child, prone to ear infections. He didn't receive proper medical care from his foster homes. Unlike the warm environs of the Rice home provided to the girls, he was not treated well at the foster home and was routinely abused both physically and emotionally. When the boy had to have ear surgery at an early age, the foster family was not expected to pay for the operation. Rice didn't have the money either. Ethel, Mary Randolph's sister, paid the $1000 for the operation; Mary Randolph was not consulted or asked for the funds. Even following the operation, David remained in Pleasant Prairie, Wisconsin in a foster placement with the family of the town plumber. Nan and Elton Rice could not care for three children properly at their age and on their income. According to Nancy, Nan Rice felt overwrought at the idea of raising a boy, since her experiences to date had been only with girls: Rice, Nancy and Iris.

Raising a second family proved difficult for the Rices. After a particularly grueling period in which both children had chicken pox and measles, Nan and Elton Rice left the girls in a foster home, a farm in

Hebron, Wisconsin. David was brought to the farm as well and stayed with his sisters. Being city children, the girls were afraid of the goats and chickens on the farm, and of the people, who seemed to lead a different lifestyle. The Wintermutens, the foster family, had been circus performers before retiring to a rural area. The couple would perform magic tricks and put on puppet shows for the children. A Christian Scientist family, they added to the children's checkered religious training. After Nan Rice recovered from the stress, the girls returned to their home with the Rices, and David went back to the foster home in Pleasant Prairie.

In 1937, Rice and Ferguson moved back to Fort Atkinson. Even though the two were not married, Nan and Elton Rice accepted Ferguson as a son-in-law, and welcomed them into their home.

While Rice didn't return to school, she kept at some of the pursuits of her younger days. A carryover from her childhood, she continued to write poetry during this period. She won several small prizes for her work, submitting it mostly to regional journals. Some of the verse made its way into small presses and anthologies. Ironically, one piece of her work, "The Immeasurables," was included in *Poetry out of Wisconsin* along with the work of another young writer, Stuart Palmer. Although they didn't meet in 1937 when the anthology was published, Palmer and Rice would become fast friends a few years later. Palmer had published two mystery novels by this point featuring his schoolteacher sleuth, Hildegarde Withers. Part of Rice's poem from that anthology follows:

> Something less than love, and more than desire,
> sweeter than dreams, yet not so sweet as sleeping,
> deeper than tears,
> lighter than laughter,
> all beauty spent and lost in the lake of fire,
> all night is drowned in the eyes like violets weeping
> quietly in the rain. And after,
> let the terrible silence strike...
>   ...Lost like a wave of the wind's making,
> gone in the cool swift rush of the forgetting hour,
> something quicker than dreams, yet not so quick as waking,

more than a blade of grass,
less than a flower,
What do I want of you, what am I seeking?
Nothing to keep, something to lose in the taking,
night skies come close
with beauty massing
purple on purple. Something beyond all speaking,
and left untold. The fragile moment is waking,
take it before it fades
in passing
as weak as a wall of wind...
    ...Lost in the night, beyond returning,
words go by like smoke, go like the last stars setting.
What of the words, with all the red night burning?
More than remembrance,
Less than forgetting,

The poem depicts Rice's rather indecisive spirit, wavering in direction. She writes about finding herself in the middle of something and not being at any extreme, an apt metaphor for her life at this point. She found herself in a relationship that wasn't marriage, but within which she had a child. She held jobs that weren't careers. Rice couldn't decide what area of writing most appealed to her. Poetry was personally satisfying to her, but no amount of verse could pay the bills. Journalism was profitable, but the pace drained most people, and didn't leave her free to travel with Ferguson. Magazine work was slower, but less certain in the days of the Depression. She began to toy with the idea of a full-length work of fiction.

Oblivious to the plight of her children, Rice continued to work as a journalist, covering areas of Wisconsin and Chicago. As part of her newspaper work as a crime reporter, she covered a local murder trial. The wily defense attorney, who had a flair for dramatic courtroom theatrics, intrigued Rice. She began thinking about the man, and playing with ideas for a book, a murder mystery like nothing ever done before. She knew that murder itself was not funny, but could be humorous through situation, tension and language. "It was simply that the situation [a trial Rice covered] had reached a point where everybody had to laugh, scream, or go crazy. That, perhaps, helps to explain why humor and homicide go hand in hand."[2] Rice was always one to see the humor in a situation, and was quick to make others laugh. She had a penchant for wild stories and exaggeration that livened up even the dullest stories. The trial provided her a chance to flex her creative muscles in a brand new way. While still living with Ferguson, she began writing her first mystery.

CHAPTER THREE

"the reading public is divided between those who read detective fiction and those who consider them trash"

By the end of World War I, the detective novel had become a puzzle book. A crime, typically murder, pitted the aristocratic sleuth against the reader and the equally well-bred villain. The form evolved into a mental combat of dilettantes from the days of Sherlock Holmes' rational methods (still unseen to many readers) to Freeman Wills Croft with his train timetables. The notion of fair play stood at the center of these novels. The reader had access to all the clues (albeit buried among arcane details) so that she might be able to solve the crime in advance of the sleuth, provided she paid attention to the red herrings and alibis. Rules, established by The Detection Club in London, and writers like S.S. Van Dine and Ronald Knox, spelled out what was permissible in the books, and what constituted a foul. No devious twins, no untraceable poisons, no supernatural, no evil Chinese genius, and no solution by intuition or accident.

These were just some of the edicts put down by the masters of the puzzle form.

No mention was made of how to handle humor in the genre. Even among the biggest stars in the field, humor was a secondary characteristic of the novel. Craig Rice pushed comedy to the forefront of the mystery world.

Three fair-play detective writers dominated Britain during the 1920s: Agatha Christie, Dorothy Sayers, and Anthony Berkeley. Of this trio, Christie made readers laugh out loud; giving us Hercule Poirot with his mangled English phraseology and studied, symmetrical vanity. Miss Marple shared village stories that seemed irrelevant to the plot, but the pertinence of the tales became clear at the end. In Sayers' early books, Lord Peter was mildly amusing as a caricature aristocrat, but as the author's skills grew, Wimsey developed into a flesh and blood character. The reader felt his pain and insecurity in wooing Harriet Vane, his troubles with sentencing criminals, and the war that haunted him. The Berkeley books were traditional puzzles, but with a sense of humor brought to them by outrageous sleuth Roger Sheringham.

With the advent of Prohibition, the Americans began to have their own noteworthy entries in the detective novel. S.S. Van Dine began writing the typical American great detective in the early 1920s. His character, Philo Vance, solved crimes through his expert knowledge of many arcane fields of study. The crimes were elaborate, and in cases where traditional proof of the crime could not bring a criminal to trial, Vance meted out his own justice to the killer. Ellery Queen (the writing team of cousins Fred Dannay and Manfred Lee), John Dickson Carr, and Rex Stout started writing a few short years after Van Dine, and helped to level the playing field between the shores. The Americans stretched the comic side of the detective story in ways that the British hadn't. Even though John Dickson Carr was born in America, many of his settings and characters closely resembled the great British detectives. Both the Carr and Carter Dickson books (Carr's pseudonym) feature larger-than-life characters, who sparked unusual developments through their own outlandish personalities. This personality-driven humor was closest in nature to Rice's own brand of hilarity. The Stout books contain the interplay between Archie and Nero Wolfe, some of the most humorous and fully drawn dialogue in mystery. The reader looked forward to the clashes between the take-no-guff assistant and the pompous, schedule-oriented Wolfe. The humor stemmed from the enormous personality gap between the characters. While Ellery Queen provided some of the most intellectually stimulating mysteries ever written, the cerebral nature of the books left little room for snickers. Queen was not a man for frivolity or mirth.

With the start of the Great Depression in 1929, and the onset of hard times and unemployment, a new, bleak reality came to America in the form of greater violence and the rise of organized crime. People lived in fear of losing their homes, their jobs, and possibly their lives if they crossed a Capone or Dillinger. A new type of crime novel came into being that reflected this loss of hope. The difference between the two forms was as great as the divide between the Rockefellers and the Hoovervilles.

The so-called hardboiled novels had their birth in the 1920s, in pulp magazines that paid small sums for stories, forcing writers to publish thousands of words to eke out a living. The pulps, presses that put out weekly or monthly magazines, featured dark, gritty stories packed with sex and violence. The magazines permitted no pretensions in this form: no affected detectives; no literary quotes, and no humor. There were no untraceable poisons, just bullets and gangsters who liked violence for its own sake, described graphically in the text.

Starting with *Red Harvest* and *The Dain Curse* in 1929, and through the course of three more novels, Dashiell Hammett changed the course of the American detective story. His realistic novels took the hardboiled stories that had appeared in pulp magazines like *The Black Mask* and raised them to a higher literary plane. Not only did he include the usual elements of corrupt police and gangsters, he added engaging plots, realistic characters with solid motivations, and vividly described backgrounds. No dilettantes, just common men who were not much different than the criminals they chased. His most famous detective, Sam Spade, had a code of ethics that he kept, though many readers would be uncomfortable operating in his moral arena.

Hammett had worked as a Pinkerton agent, and the realism shows in his work. Sam Spade, in *The Maltese Falcon*, represented a far different detective than Wimsey or Poirot. He made his living solving crimes, outside of the bureaucracy and police corruption. The policemen in his world were adversaries, not foils. Hammett's books rose above the plot - the puzzle, as it were, and that allowed the reader to re-read the novel. Many of the Golden Age books would only be read once, as the convoluted plot was the entire reason for the book. The characters and prose could not sustain another glance without the author's tricky sleight-of-hand.

The success of Hammett's novels started a whole group of imitators, private detectives who drank and killed as they tried to solve a case. His books also developed the notion of the tarnished knight walking the mean streets of the city. Raymond Chandler, another American whose work is frequently compared to Hammett's, romanticized the concept of the chivalrous private eye with a code of ethics beyond that of the streets. His first novel, *The Big Sleep*, came out the same year as Rice's first novel, *8 Faces at 3*. Chandler's work was less gritty and more stylistic than Hammett's. Where Hammett would destroy cities or societies to rebuild them, Chandler's heroes walked amongst the filthy without getting dirty. Philip Marlowe, his protagonist/private eye, represented an idealized hero, someone who solved crimes and fought injustice while remaining untouched by the corruption around him.

Like Hammett's, Chandler's work centered more on writing style and mechanics than complicated whodunits. Chandler detested the Emily Post style of mystery, as he referred to it. While some of the two authors' plots are as deceptive as anything from the Golden Age, their concentration focused on the actual language, the crisp dialogue and the descriptions. The seamier side of life, the poverty and decay that had blanketed America in the 1930s, was exposed to the reader through brilliant prose. Chandler's work stood apart from many of his contemporaries. Even today, his work is the subject of doctoral studies in literature.

With the advent of the hardboiled school, humor was as dead as Sam Spade's partner. Few chuckles could exist in the violent world of these detectives. Hammett's books afforded few laughs, although wise-cracks did appear in some of Chandler's work. The situational humor and the comic characters that had been prevalent in the Golden Age books disappeared.

Onto this scene burst Craig Rice like a screwball comedy in the midst of the Cannes Film Festival. Her books would have to be labeled hardboiled in the sense that her protagonist is a criminal lawyer in private practice, hired to investigate crimes for his clients. The people expected in a hardboiled mystery populate the books: Mafia, crooked aldermen, bartenders, and shady dealers. But even if a character was a threat, he still had a likable side to him, a comic twist that made him endearing. Rice also included the upper crust of Chicago polite society, a people who lived to consume alcohol and to party. The novels lacked the violence, and gritty feel of the streets. Mostly Rice's novels defy categorization, a humorous twist on the murder mystery.

In *The Art of the Mystery Story*, Rice admitted she didn't know what attributes made her books so funny. The novels were humorous in the same manner as Rice herself: manic; witty; and a touch sarcastic. She listed some of the comedic literary devices used in her time: "There is the device of peppering an otherwise plain-and-honest mystery story with so many brilliant wisecracks that every now and then the reader doesn't know if he is reading about murder or listening to Fred Allen. That, for the writer, is the easy method, provided he is smart enough to think up the wisecracks or knows a lot of witty friends and carries a notebook.

"There is the device of larding an otherwise heavy story with a couple of quaint bucolic characters who go around stumbling and bumbling and getting in everybody's way, and, at intervals, emitting gems of earthy wisdom until you can't see the plot for the platitudes.

"Then there is the situation of the humorously bungling policeman. This is sure-fire stuff. Practically everyone in this vale of tears and jeers has, at some time in his life, been scared by and/or mad at a policeman. Therefore, to make a fool of a cop is all that the mystery novel detective has to do to make himself a hero."[1]

Although Rice never revealed in the article what device made her own books so appealing, she used a mixture of the items listed therein and more. Her characters can be extremely witty and charming. Malone forever mangles platitudes, making a philosophical malapropism give a new slant on the subject. "'Never mind, Maggie', the lawyer said, "no use crying over spilled clients.'"[2] "Pride goeth before the spring. I mean, pride springeth into fall. I mean, spring—"[3] Malone's unorthodox logic always makes a twisted kind of sense.

Likewise, some of Rice's characters get in everyone's way. The detective team of Bingo Riggs and Handsome Kuzak always land in the middle of a plot that they just don't quite understand, or a situation that began years prior to the duo's entrance. The police think anyone silly enough to get involved must know something, and the villains want them out of the way. Still, they resolve their predicaments with a few more dollars in their pockets. Many plots of the later Rice books turn on instances in which a character's interrupted confession (or unasked questions) doesn't tell something that could have solved the murder chapters ago.

Certainly, not even the most generous reader could consider Daniel von Flanagan a credible policeman. He tells anyone who'll listen that he didn't want to be a cop; this was merely a repaid political favor. He takes each murder personally, as though crimes were committed to make his life more difficult. The overworked cop added the "von" to his name to prevent people from characterizing him as the typical dumb Irish cop. His penchant for new careers is almost as mind-boggling as Rice's. Nor can he be considered good at this job. Overwhelmed by Helene Justus' charm and beauty, the policeman can never stay mad at her, no matter what her crimes.

However, one of the most appealing aspects of the Rice books is the "Gee, whiz" attitude of her protagonists, especially her most famous trio: Jake, Helene, and Malone. The buoyant, can't-be-beat attitude bounds off the page at the reader, letting him or her know that everything will work out before the last chapter. They'll have a fun time getting there; no matter how bad things look for the heroes. These characters come across as children who never grew up, Peter Pan lost on the streets of the Windy City. Without responsibility, the trio's only task is to have fun, toss back a few ryes, and find the killer.

The first of the Rice novels featuring John J. Malone, Jake Justus and Helene Brand, *8 Faces at 3*, was published in 1939. While the book is not one of Craig's best efforts (as most first novels aren't), *8 Faces* contains many of the characteristic elements associated with Rice novels. The opening chapter sets the scene by introducing an impossible or dire situation. Rice's works typically contained a first chapter set apart from the rest of the book, a strong narrative hook that lured the reader before introducing the protagonists or the familiar details. Rice knew from working in advertising and public relations that the reader had to be drawn into the work. In the first chapter of *8 Faces at 3*, Holly Inglehart awakens from claustrophobic nightmares to discover herself alone in her great-aunt's mansion with a very dead Aunt Alex. All the clocks have been stopped at 3 a.m., and Alexandra Inglehart has been murdered, with Holly the only other person in the room. "The room whirled around, she [Holly] felt herself sinking into some unknown darkness, the darkness that had oppressed her in the dream. But as consciousness fled from her in a rushing stream, one last thing struck into her mind.

"The clock.

"The clock, Aunt Alex's little French clock in its little bell glass. The little wheel above the clock that had always whirled back and forth, all day long and all night long. It was not whirling now.

"The fragile, gilded hands stood at three o'clock."[4]

Rice would recount in letters that the first chapter had come to her in a dream. She later admitted in an article for *The Writer* that she had written the first chapter, but then didn't know what to do next. The opening had stumped her as well. "I wrote it [the first chapter] down, quick like a bunny, and then discovered it was baffling... It was eighteen months before I got up enough courage to begin Chapter Two..."[5] When Rice did finally sit down to write a book, it was a sight to see. Her writing habits were legendary. She wrote without an outline, or character sketches, or any good idea of where she was going, simply typing away until she'd completed a novel. The manic sessions would sometimes last for days. These focused writing sessions provided the first indication that perhaps Craig Rice didn't behave like other writers - she was driven to complete a work in a few settings. No one would see her until she emerged with a finished book.

Although John J. Malone would become the star of later books and appear solo in most of the short stories, Jake Justus appeared as the viewpoint character in this first novel. He is the character brought into the murder, and the one who solves the mystery. Jake was "a tall, rangy man, big-boned and lean with an indolent slouch. Under an untidy thatch of red hair was an angular, friendly face with watchful eyes and a square jaw. There were a few wrinkles on his face too."[6] The redheaded, ex-newspaper-reporter-turned-press-agent for Dick Dayton, was the driving force in trying to clear Holly, Mrs. Dick Dayton, of the murder charges. In comparing Rice to her characters, most reviewers have likened her to Helene, the beautiful blonde; however, in many respects (with the obvious exception of gender), Rice resembles Jake more. The reader learns that Jake is an orphan from a small town who goes through a variety of jobs, including public relations and newspaper reporting, before landing a career that appeals to him.

Helene is almost the antithesis of Jake. Raised by her wealthy parents in the posh Chicago suburb of Maple Park, she never had to work a day in her life. An heiress, Helene's money causes more than a few problems for the couple. Jake's pride reflects the mores of the day, that a self-respecting man didn't take money from a woman, even his wife. In contrast to Jake's rumpled, friendly looks, Helene is described as a cool beauty, "made of ice and steel. Her hair was ash blonde, almost white, combed sleekly back from her ivory-pale, finely modeled face. Her eyes were blue and brilliant. She was dressed informally in galoshes, fur coat, and blue satin house pajamas."[7] Though more of a bon vivant, Helene's persona mirrors more accurately Mary Randolph (Rice's mother) than Rice herself. The reviewers forgot that this mystery writer had taken a man's name as a pseudonym early in her career, and stereotypically made the comparison solely based on the author's gender. No one who knew Craig Rice would describe her as a cool beauty.

Into the dichotomy of Jake and Helene comes John J. Malone, described as: "A contractor, or a barkeep, or a baseball manager. Something like that. At first sight he was not impressive. He was short, heavy—though not fat—with thinning dark hair and a red, perspiring face that grew more red and more perspiring as he talked. He was an untidy man; the press of his suits usually suggested that he had been sleeping in them, probably on the floor of a taxicab. His ties and collars never became really close friends, often not even acquaintances. Most of the buttons on his vest were undone, and almost invariably he had one shoelace untied."[8] The lawyer is said to be a master of courtroom pyrotechnics, and yet, in the entire Rice canon, he never practices law inside of a courtroom. He claims never to have lost a client, and goes well beyond the call of duty to save Holly Inglehart Dayton as he unmasks the real killer. He helps Holly escape from the police, and hides her as he buys some time to learn the truth.

Another trait of Rice's books is that the typical Malone client has no parents, and was likely taken in by relatives. Holly Inglehart proves no exception to this rule. Holly's mother died in childbirth. Her father ran off, leaving Holly and her brother, Glen, in the care of an aunt who threatened to disinherit Holly should she ever marry. "Her sister - my mother - had married foolishly and broken Aunt Alex's heart, and I wasn't to be allowed to marry at all. It was - well, a kind of repayment. I was to stay single and live with Aunt Alex as long as she lived, and take care of her. She told me that she'd left her money tied up so that I wouldn't inherit anything if I married after her death."[9] Left in that stifling environment, Holly tried to thrive while Glen festered. Years earlier, Aunt Alex had interfered to halt a romance between Glen and Helene Brand. The older woman had blackmailed Helene into breaking off the relationship because of an embarrassing (but unnamed) incident in the Helene's past. Even the cool heiress demurs at mentioning details.

Again, years later in *The Lucky Stiff*, Craig wrote about a girl left at birth and the pain the character endured.

"'You're the one who's been doing the hating, as long as you could remember. You hated your father for deserting your mother. You hated the people in Grove Junction who had all the things you wanted. You hated grandmother, because all she left was a mortgaged house, a garnet necklace, and a pair of silver earrings. . . Other girls had things you wanted. . . Expensive clothes, and a house without a mortgage. And dates with boys whose parents approved of them. I can understand why you hated them.'"[10]

In her essay on Craig Rice in the anthology *And Then There Were Nine... More Women of Mystery*, Peggy Moran details the scant histories of the main characters in the Rice novels. Of the detective triumvirate who populates the majority of Rice's novels, only Helene meets a parental figure. George Brand, Helene's father, makes an appearance in *The Wrong Murder*. A manservant accompanies him, but no mention is ever made of a mother figure in the canon. A black cloud envelopes Mrs. Brand. The reader must assume that Helene's mother divorced George, or died, because he later involves himself with a woman that Helene thinks wants George's fortune, although Helene seems not to care. Rice explores Jake's family superficially in *Trial By Fury*, and Malone's background varies by story, with the overall impression that he grew up in an orphanage, dumped by parents for unknown reasons. Yet, despite the orphan-effect's intrusion into virtually every book, Rice denied that being abandoned as a child had made an impression on her.

As mentioned, the book contains many of the problems inherent in a first novel. The book foreshadows too much and too frequently. From the first chapter, there can be no mistake that *8 Faces* is a crime novel, and the references to forthcoming events distract the reader. The novel is also one of Rice's most weakly plotted, in that the whole scheme would fall apart if a character had bothered to look at a wristwatch.

Simon & Schuster mystery editor, Lee Wright, shared, "I accepted the manuscript of *8 Faces at 3*, Craig Rice's first novel, on the basis of fifty pages and found out later that it had been turned down by some twelve publishers. What foolish people there are in the world! ...Her people were so appealing that even Craig had the devil's own time selecting the murderer."[11]

Rice's own personal life did not settle down with the publication of her first novel. Her relationship with Ferguson faltered. Ferguson's health weakened, and with the publication of her novel, Rice's attention went a million other places, none in the direction of her companion. Rice went back to Fort Atkinson and stayed with her adoptive parents and children. Upset with Rice's behavior towards Ferguson, Nan Rice insisted that Rice's place was with Ferguson, especially when he needed her.

As Rice settled in with her new notoriety in 1939, Ferguson took a trip to California to visit some relatives. Shortly after his return,

Ferguson suffered a fatal heart attack. Ironically, his death certificate stated that he had separated from his wife, Craig Rice. Rice had been visiting Nan and Elton Rice in Fort Atkinson at the time, and wasn't with Ferguson at his death. When Ferguson died, Rice decided to leave David in the foster home in Pleasant Prairie. The boy had traveled with Ferguson on occasion to Washington to visit the Ferguson family, but upon Ferguson's death, David remained in Wisconsin full-time.

Rice didn't last long without a romance. From the time she was eighteen, she always managed to have a love interest that she intended to marry or had wed. Craig would later tell friends that she attended a Chicago literary party on the arm of one man, met Lawrence Lipton, and left with him. Lipton wooed her with long letters that still showed the unconventional mindset of the two authors. "Well, we did say somethin' about love and all - sorta unbeknownst to ourself, but god-dam it all, gents, it was the night of the full moon, the sun hadn't risen for days, strange signs and wonders had been observed all week along Huron street [sic], all the plate glass windows on Michigan avenue [sic] had been shattered by an explosion of unknown origin only an hour before,"[12]

Rice met Lipton in late 1939, and married him in 1940. Lipton was another writer who took his career (and himself) very seriously. He was short, balding, and of Jewish descent, born in Poland and moving to Chicago as a youngster. Alarmingly liberal for even the Rices, Lipton belonged to the Communist party, and displayed his party card as a badge of honor at casual get-togethers.

Lipton's pretensions were not well received by the family. Jesse Young, Rice's aunt, bought the new couple a plastic knife as a wedding present for the much-married bride. Rice was Lipton's third wife, so he had little room to talk in the matrimony department. Rice showed her usual inquisitive nature about the new product, and laughed at the gift, which would probably outlast many weddings, but the present perplexed the groom. His sense of humor didn't allow him to laugh at himself and he quickly alienated himself from most of Rice's family.

Despite the differences in temperament, Rice and Lipton shared a great deal in common. They both loved to entertain and invite friends to the apartment. People talked about their parties for days afterwards. Among the guests at the new apartment were the many

Sherlock Holmes fans in the Chicago area. The Baker Street Irregulars comprised the only organized mystery group in the late 1930s. Unlike today's many conventions and organizations, in the years before World War II, sherlockiana was the only group dedicated to mystery (Mystery Writers of America would not exist for another six years). Vincent Starrett, one of the most respected Holmesians and author of *Sherlock Holmes of Baker Street*, lived in Chicago. As a good public relations person, Rice made his acquaintance to promote her book. She was introduced to the mystery buffs in the city, who took her under their wing and initiated her into the mystery world. Ben Abramson, another Holmes buff, mailed *8 Faces at 3* to mystery fans across the country. Rice met the bookstore owners in the area who stocked her book and gave her first novel a push. The humorous content in a time of Europe's war made it a welcome, if unorthodox, entry into mystery fiction.

Rice's work in the field of public relations paid off for her. Long before conventional wisdom dictated the need to sign books and network, she made a habit of it. She sought out collectors, bookstores, and reviewers. She entertained fans in her home. She partied with Chicago society and met people who might help a young author. Mystery organizations like Sisters-in-Crime would not be established for another forty years to help writers accomplish these same goals. Rice's public enjoyed the first madcap adventure set in Chicago and didn't have to wait long for the next.

CHAPTER FOUR

"and of course Gypsy Rose Lee (whose G-String Murders sold nearly 30,000 copies)."

R ice's second novel with Simon & Schuster hit the stands just months after her first book. Originally entitled Between Broadcasts, the contracts for *The Corpse Steps Out* were inked only a couple of months following those for *8 Faces at 3*. Since Nelle Brown, the major non-series character in *The Corpse Steps Out* appears as Jake's lone client in the final pages of Rice's first novel, Rice most likely wrote both books in the same time span. She enjoyed sharing characters between books, and sometimes between series.

The Corpse Steps Out epitomizes Rice's Malone mysteries in more ways than her first attempt at the genre. The book, set in a Chicago area radio station, resembles the station that employed Rice while she wrote this book. While *8 Faces* had been set mostly at the rather non-descript Inglehart mansion in Maple Park, Rice's subsequent works would be set against a variety of fascinating backdrops and professions, all of which could be traced back to her own life. Rice's own experiences varied so much that a multitude of murder stories could be written using the backgrounds.

In addition to the radio station setting, downtown Chicago inside the Loop became a major component in the Rice novels. The reader gets a feel for the streets of the Windy City as Helene navigates them in her convertible or as Malone finds a bar to drown his sorrows.

"She turned onto a side street, turned again, and drove up an alley, made another turn, and entered the labyrinth of underground passages known as the lower level. Skillfully, she maneuvered the big car into the cavernous street that was directly below Michigan Avenue and drove straight to the double-decker bridge. It was still up and she paused at the barrier."[1]

The plot for *The Corpse Steps Out* could be the script for a screwball comedy, almost as wild as Helene's driving. In his career as press agent/manager, Jake is down to a single client, Nelle Brown, who is being blackmailed over an indiscreet love affair. Afraid of being bounced by the radio station's moral turpitude clause, Nelle asks for Jake's help when she finds her lover's dead body. Additionally, Nelle is married to an older man who went crazy because of the loss of his fortune. Her husband sees horses in their house, and imagines that strange men are following Nelle. Like Rice, Nelle married a much older man. In what will be a typical Rice touch, Nelle's husband is called Tootz. Rice's mother, Mary, was nicknamed Tootz, or "T" for short. Indeed, Rice makes Tootz the villain of the piece, another lingering indication of her antipathy towards her birth mother. The specter of Mary (who was also used as a model for Helene) is never far from Rice's writing.

At the start of the book, Jake encounters Helene (who had left him a year and a half earlier). The reader is surprised to find out that the couple had split up immediately following the end of *8 Faces at 3*. They had seemed destined to be together, but Helene's money had come between them. Now they quickly work out their issues. "There she stood, as patrician, as beautiful, as perfect as ever, in the midst of the noontime crowd on Michigan Avenue. Her pale blond hair was exquisite in place, and she was dressed simply in a very low-cut pale-violet chiffon evening gown. She was carrying a Parma violet evening wrap. And she was not sober."[2] Reunited, the constant interruptions by clients, missing bodies, arson, the police and virtually every citizen of

Chicago prevent Jake and Helene from getting married.

Much like a screwball comedy, the blend is appealing, but illogical. Paul March is murdered, and then his body disappears. So do the letters he had proving his affair with Nelle. Jake finds no trace of the murder when he goes to investigate. The body re-appears, only to disappear again. After the death of Paul March, the murderer shoots a soap producer with a similar modus operandi, and likewise a blackmailing John St. John. The bodies shift like the ball in a shell game. Tootz's warehouse is destroyed by arson. The bodies disappear and reappear with such frequency that Daniel von Flanagan contemplates becoming a mink farmer.

The subtle shift towards Malone as sleuth starts in this book. Rice found it easier (as many authors do) to have a professional as the sleuth. That way, clients can come to him for help, and not stretch the reader's credulity that a pair of amateurs could continue to fall over bodies. Malone is touted as the brain who can solve any case. "John Joseph Malone would handle it. Malone would find a way." [3] Indeed, Malone identifies the murderer from scant clues, but the readers are so busy catching their breath at the end of the book that Rice's slim clues can be overlooked. Much like screwball comedies didn't follow the rules of drama, Rice felt no need to comply with the rules of the Detection Club.

Rice published a second book in 1940, *The Wrong Murder*. That made three Malone-Justus novels in just over a year. Rice was on a roll, and putting out books at a pace that most writers couldn't match. She had pretty much abandoned the rest of her freelance work at this point, and dedicated herself to writing mystery novels.

In a gutsy move, Rice informed the reader in the title that a particular character (who should be the primary suspect) didn't commit the crime. Mona McLane, Chicago socialite and oft-married woman, makes a bet with Jake during the reception after his wedding to Helene. "I'll commit a murder and you pin it on me. I'll bet you can't do it. I'll bet you ... the Casino." [4]

When someone shoots a man at the corner of State and Madison, Jake and Helene assume that Joshua Gumbril died by Mona's hand, and vow to prove her guilty. Mona had vowed to commit the murder in a very public place, and the location of the shooting definitely fit the bill. The couple read the description of the dead man in the newspaper the day after their wedding.

"His first appearance on State Street that could be proved beyond a shadow of a doubt was at the northwest corner of Van Buren, just below the steps leading to the elevated. He had paused briefly to buy a newspaper. The newsstand boy remembered him clearly, especially the manner in which he had fished the depths of a worn leather change purse for the odd penny.

"Then they found the little man later in the day, the newspaper was still tucked under his arm unread, just as the boy had folded it.

"No one would have expected him to be noticed anywhere, especially not on State Street in the last week before Christmas. He was a trifle under the average height, stoop-shouldered, and exceedingly thin."[5]

Money matters still divide the couple, specifically Jake's lack and Helene's surplus. Jake's only client, Nelle Brown, has left town, exacerbating the situation. Despite Jake's unemployment, he and Helene are married at the beginning of the book. Between jobs, Jake wants to win the Casino to put him on an equal footing with his wife. One wonders if Jake's obsession stemmed in part from Rice's family situation. Her growing reputation, and Lipton's relative obscurity, made for tense moments on the homefront. Rice's popularity and the increasing sales of her rapid output of books made her a minor celebrity. Lipton's published works consisted of a few poems and essays, and he didn't stand a chance of competing with his successful wife.

In *The Wrong Murder* and other Rice novels, secret knowledge and blackmail play a vital part in the plot. Gumbril collected information about the people around him. All the documentation, which he stored in a small box, disappeared shortly after his audacious murder. Malone and the honeymoon couple decide to determine who had the most to lose by the revelations in the cache, and investigate Mona's acquaintances.

The Chicago retinue assisting Malone is introduced in this book. Max Hook, the head of Chicago's gambling syndicate, lost the Casino to Mona on a bet. Hook owns an apartment building on Lake Shore Drive, a prestigious address he takes pride in decorating to his sensibilities. As often as von Flanagan changes dream careers, Max Hook changes color schemes. "The living room was immense, rose-carpeted, filled with delicately carved, satin-upholstered furniture, with innumerable little decorative lamps, pink-shaded, and with what seemed to be hundreds upon hundreds of small silk pillows."[6] While he keeps a scarred desk as a constant reminder of his past and his career, the rest of the penthouse goes from modern to French Provincial with stops along the way.

With Hook, the author introduces several other underworld figures. His henchman, Little Georgie "the Cherry" la Cerra, learns to respect Helene after an impromptu drive through the wintry downtown streets. Maggie, Malone's long-suffering secretary, makes her first appearance in this book as well. For the first several books, she only answers to her name, has participates in little dialogue. At best, in the early novels, she rolls her eyes and manages to survive on whatever and whenever Malone pays her.

The only parental figure of the detective trio appears in *The Wrong Murder*. George Brand, Helene's father, attends Helene's wedding accompanied by his manservant, Partridge. Traveling from Hawaii to Florida, the two men stopped by for a visit. "There stood Partridge, a small, thin, grayish man, with perpetually anxious eyes. Jake had long since given up trying to decide if he were George Brand's valet or his legal guardian. He always seemed to be just on the verge of some disapproving comment, which was never actually spoken. He seemed especially on the verge of some such comment now, though all he managed was one little, reproachful, and infinitely sad cough."[7] George Brand's antics make it easy to see where Helene gets her irrepressible humor, as George manages to swap facial hair with another man and drinks his daughter under the table.

Real life copied fiction when Bosco Craig returned to the United States in 1940 for the first time in almost thirty years. He didn't meet his long lost daughter until the following year. A stranger to these people who bore his likeness, he had multiple sons-in-law and three grandchildren by the start of World War II. In the intervening years in Asia, he had married Laura Guerite, an Australian music hall performer. His time had been spent in the Orient; traveling in India, Hong Kong, and Tokyo as a businessman. Without Mary Randolph's influence and money, Bosco Craig had abandoned his art training. As imperial Japan became increasingly aggressive in the Pacific area in the late 1930s (a precursor to World War II), Craig decided to bring his wife back to the relative safety of the United States. However, the Japanese captured the Craigs, and traded them, among others, to the United States in a prisoner exchange. Though Rice heard about the exchange and her father's return to the States, Bosco Craig didn't hurry to his daughter's side.

Rice's non-encounter with her father shows up in her next book. A character with a casual similarity to Rice's father appears in *The Right Murder*, which came out in early 1941. Actually, three characters, all named Gerald Tuesday, bear a striking resemblance to Bosco Craig. While Craig's career in the Orient wasn't as rough as the Tuesday brothers', likenesses exist: they were cut off for years from their family, trading in commodities, and resided in the Orient. The Tuesdays were strangers to their kin, just as Craig was to Rice.

This book also raised an issue that wasn't spoken of in the 1940s-the physical abuse of a spouse. Rice became one of the first mystery authors to moralize about social issues in her books. Michael Venning routinely beat his wife, Editha, and received his own punishment for that offense by the end of the book. "Editha Venning showed no signs of her experience of the night before and wore a show of outward calm, but the light in her eyes was almost a glitter, and two spots of color burned high on her cheeks."[8] "The dreamy look came into Malone's eyes again. "She was justified if anyone ever was," he began. "...was not only defending herself against bullets when she killed him, but against the intolerable condition of -"[9] While many of the hardboiled mysteries dealt with the evils of society, their male authors, wrote of issues concerning societal justice and crime. Not issues that pertained to women. Rice included these issues in her work, taking the books to a more emotional level and attracting more female readers, who could relate to stories that matched their every day lives.

The book opens with Malone missing his two friends and a long-legged brunette from Chez Paree. He spends his time commiserating with Joe the Angel, better known as Joe deAngelo, who owns Joe the Angel's City Hall Bar on Dearborn, in the Loop. Joe knows everything that goes on in the city; however, no political figure, save the city hall janitor, ever passes through his door. While he's drowning his sorrows in Joe's bar, the first of the Gerald Tuesdays locates Malone and slips him a key before dying. When another corpse shows up, also with the name of Gerald Tuesday, Malone decides to get to the bottom of the murders. Before the end of the case, a third man named Gerald Tuesday enters the scene.

There was another similarity to Rice's own life in this novel: her relationship with Lipton turned sour early on. The pair engaged in huge rows, and Rice suffered physical abuse on more than one occasion. Lipton had rigid ideas about the family structure. Combined with alcohol, the family situation grew toxic. Because of her own separation anxieties, Rice found it nearly impossible to leave him. Sadly, she received physical abuse past the end of 1941, and was not saved like Editha at the end of *The Right Murder*.

Rice completed the switch to Malone as a viewpoint character in *The Right Murder*. Part of the reason for the switch involved plot logistics. Jake and Helene briefly split up after their honeymoon to separately solve Mona's bet and win the Casino for each other. As the couple operates in different parts of the city, (Helene takes up residence with Mona while Jake stays at their apartment), the situational humor would be lessened by the use of only Jake's viewpoint. Malone tries to keep the couple apart until he can solve the murder and reunite them with the deed to the nightclub.

A series rarely switches viewpoint characters over the course of several books in mystery fiction. Only rarely does a character take over the stage from the designated protagonist. Typically, one character remains front and center for the life of the series. If a new character is wanted, or the current sleuth bores the author, a new series is created in a different milieu. The shift is made subtly here, not in one book but over a series of three books, so the change is less noticeable. Patrick Quentin did this in the 1950s with the Peter Duluth series, when the Lt. Trant took over as protagonist after meeting Duluth in one of the books. However, the number of times that this has happened can be counted on one hand.

Although the killings attributed to Mona in the title have nothing to do with the ones discovered by Malone and the Justuses, the public did not issue the hue and cry made over Rice's book as they had with *The Murder of Roger Ackroyd*. By all rights the titular killer had to be Mona, but in a sense this was again the wrong murder because Mona did not kill the Tuesdays.

The detective farce novels refused to conform to the same 'play-fair with the reader' standards as straight detective novels. Rice could mislead the readers with a title, and still earn their affection. Her books were taken as a fun read for a nation worried about war in Europe, a misleading puzzle, but nothing more. Smiles would be rationed along with sugar and rubber, and Rice ran her own black market.

By now, Rice's prodigious output became well known throughout the mystery community. Today's publishing standards for genre writers call for one book a year, or less. Rice routinely wrote two or three books a year. In her excitement over her new profession, and having found her niche, she stayed up for days at a time, writing. There was no reason yet to suspect any underlying condition responsible for these bouts of writing. Her desire to produce had a manic quality to it, and annoyed Lipton immensely. The constant clack of the keys drove him to distraction. She used an old typewriter with carbons, and would emerge from her room to eat with black smudges on her face and arms.

Writing without an outline or notes, Rice used her imagination and intelligence to keep her plots clear. *Trial By Fury*, considered her best Malone work, marked Rice's fifth Malone book in three years. The book holds a place as one of two Rice works on the Haycraft-Queen Definitive Library list. Ironically, *Trial* takes place outside of familiar Chicago environs, in the small town of Jackson, Wisconsin.

When Jake and Helene go to a small town for a belated honeymoon, they look for a fishing license at the county courthouse. Just as they arrive, an ex-Senator is shot and killed. Rather than delve into the motives of the locals, the sheriff decides to lock up Jake for the murder. "Jake saw Helene opening her mouth to speak, and tightened his hand on her arm. That was exactly what he'd been thinking. These people all knew each other. They, he and Helene, were the strangers, the outlanders. He knew that everyone in the corridor was staring at them with cold, unfriendly eyes, that the two of them had been set apart from the others, standing alone and regarded with suspicion."[10] Helene calls Malone to bail out her new husband. Malone starts talking to people in town and learns that many of the residents had a reason to see the Senator dead. Jake disappears shortly afterwards, and the hilarious chase is on to find a murderer and the missing Jake.

With the Justuses out of the city, the reader is more able to see them function as a couple. Helene, raised in exclusive Maple Park, expects the people in the small town to behave like her socialite friends. For the first time, the reader truly comprehends Jake's concerns about the differences in their backgrounds. Jake knows how money can change people and relationships; Helene takes cash as a given in her universe. Reverting, Jake fills the shoes of the viewpoint character, comparing Jackson to the small town where he grew up. Without Malone's presence, Jake becomes the de-facto protagonist. His subsequent disappearance allows Malone to take back the reins of narration.

Rice's best books combine the traits of the humor that has come to be associated with her and an added personal touch. Rice modeled *Trial By Fury* on her life in Fort Atkinson with the Rices. Philomen Smith portrayed the county clerk, reflecting Elton Rice's job in Jefferson. Roy Schmidt, a real-life city hall janitor in Fort Atkinson, was the model for Buttonholes, the janitor who gave Jake and Helene an alibi when ex-Senator Pevely was shot.

Rice even used the local sights, renaming the Wayside tavern as the Den. By changing the names, Rice detailed her own life in a small town to give *Trial* a sense of realism that had been lacking in *Wrong and Right Murders*.

Although orphans and abandoned children had become a constant theme in her work, the number of women in *Trial By Fury* who had been affected by their fathers astounds the reader. Virtually every woman in the book shows the effects of poor paternal parenting. Florence Pevely described her father, the first victim in *Trial*. "I mean just plain stinker. He wasn't only an unprincipled businessman and a crooked politician, he was a stinker. . . He practically murdered my mother. Yes he did. He was so mean to her that she took poison. Everybody thought it was heart trouble. She should have given it to him."[11]

Part of this can be attributed to the return of Rice's own father to her life. Character Ellen McGowan protects her father's name in the community by going to great lengths to cover up his misdeeds. Arlene Goudge finds herself forced to hide her romantic relationships with men from her overprotective father, and the reader assumes that her unplanned pregnancy stems from these attitudes.

These characters feel drawn from flesh and blood, not caricature. *Trial By Fury* boasts no affected characters that whimsically change their behavior, names, or home decor from book to book. Mostly from putting up with the ex-Senator, her father, Florence Pevely grew up without a mother, and the effects of that loss show in her character in real ways. "That's what made me sore. I've got to get away as fast as I can. I'm neurotic, you know. Very neurotic. I wish I could tell you how much money I've spent on doctors, and they all tell me the same thing. Very neurotic. Are you surprised, living in a place like this?"[12]

The novel cuts close to Rice's own experiences in Fort Atkinson; yet Rice felt compelled to add excessive drinking. The excessive drinking by the characters marks the one low point in the novel. In one particular instance, Malone gets falling down drunk on Dollar Gin, and a bloodhound drags him across a field while trying to locate the missing Jake. "He looked around for a park bench for several minutes. While he was looking, a bird suddenly rose from the deep grass of the ditch beside the road, startling them both. Hercules gave a joyous yelp and started in the direction the bird had taken, dragging Malone after him, entangling both of them in the leash, and finally landing them in a confused heap in the bottom of a ditch." [13]

While spending so much time writing in 1940 and 1941, Rice had little time for family life. Nancy and Iris continued to live with the elder Rices in Fort Atkinson. Despite the short stay in 1939, Rice was an infrequent visitor to her children at this stage of her career. Her daughters were very like the author. At ages eleven and twelve, the girls had grown into bright, inquisitive young women. Showing the same spirit and intelligence that Rice had, they attended Hoard Elementary School under the guidance of Nan and Elton Rice. Their education were more standardized than their mother's, although Elton Rice frequently read aloud to the children, instilling a love of learning in them.

Perhaps because they had each other, the girls didn't exhibit the same separation anxiety that Rice had experienced. Nancy and Iris could leave the Rices to attend school. In February of 1941, Elton Rice passed away. By this time Craig Rice hadn't visited her family in so long that Nancy had to have someone point out her mother at the funeral.

Rice stayed in Fort Atkinson with Nan Rice for a short period of time. While she was there, she convinced her adoptive mother to move to Los Angeles to be with the Liptons, who planned to relocate in the near future.

Larry Lipton took this time of bereavement to badger Rice's agent to help sell his own works.

"Craig and I got word Saturday (last) that her foster-father-uncle, Elton Rice was dead up in Fort Atkinson. We went up there and attended the funeral, which took place on Wednesday. I got back to Chicago last night (Thursday) and Craig is staying up in Fort Atkinson till Sunday. I got your letter (of February 14) up in Fort, where it was forwarded to me, and, on returning to Chicago found Ann's letter to Craig, which I forwarded to her. Craig will be back in Chicago by Monday, so please continue to address her here if you have any occasion to write to her, and I will remain in Chicago too - if you should have any occasion to write to me, which God grant.

Concerning the matter of "impatience," Margot, does it seem like ants in the pants to enquire what gives after a publisher has had a book under consideration for five weeks (since Jan. 17), especially since he asked for "three more days" on Feb. 10 - nearly two weeks ago?"[14]

Bereaved, Nan Rice sold the house in Fort Atkinson and moved the small family to La Jolla. In California, she, Nancy, and Iris stayed with her sister in the house where Craig Rice had first realized her love of writing. After living with Mame Young for a short time, Mrs. Rice and the girls moved to Los Angeles, and rented a small apartment in Hollywood. Living in a seedy area of Los Angeles, they were afraid to go outside after dark, and sometimes during the day. The three scraped by on Nan Rice's meager social security checks and waited for Rice's arrival.

Rice continued to live in Chicago, not rushing to meet her family in California. She was busy stirring up a hurricane in the Windy City. Her famous friendship with Gypsy Rose Lee took most of her concentration. By the early forties, Lee toured the country as the America's favorite burlesque stripper. The country couldn't get enough of the entertainer. Rice spent most nights drinking and partying on Rush Street as one of Chicago's most famous residents. It was inevitable that they should meet and hit it off. Rice was a charming woman who was always the life of your party. Gypsy Rose Lee lived for a number of months in Chicago playing in Mike Todd's nightclub during 1940 and 1941. Although Rice listed a turn as Lee's publicist to *Time* reporters, no record exists of a professional relationship, just the mutual friendship of two free spirits. In a review for *Trial By Fury*, Lee tells readers about her friendship with Rice. "Craig Rice wrote part of *Trial By Fury* in my house in the country, rather in my trailer in the woods, behind my house in the country [in Highland Mills, NY], and I like to think that Bill, my dachshund, is the pattern for Hercules."[15] The pair visited each other, and enjoyed the notoriety of their respective careers.

Although Lee had written columns and short works prior to the war, her friendship with Rice most likely sparked the idea to write her own mystery novel. Despite their relationship, Rice apparently did not ghostwrite *The G-String Murders*. Still, no talk of Rice's canon would be complete without a complete discussion of those rumors. In many publications, the books are explicitly listed as part of Rice's work. The rumors started before publication that someone else had ghostwritten Lee's novel, and Rice came to mind first in conjunction with the mystery. She and Lee were two of the most famous residents of Chicago, and friends besides. Adding to the rumor, Lee and Rice shared the same editor (Lee Wright) at Simon & Schuster. Like the snafu with her name, Rice, who laughed at the various inaccuracies of the press, didn't bother to correct the assumption.

Although Lee's style bears superficial similarities to Rice's, distinct differences in mechanics exist. Lee had spent several months living in Brooklyn Heights at 7 Middagh Street in the early months of 1940, at the home of George Davis, who was the fiction editor at *Harper's Bazaar*. Davis had trouble paying the rent, and several authors moved in to make the residence their home. The address boasted several influential writers who moved in and out over the course of a month, including Louis MacNiece, Carson McCullers, W.H. Auden, and Christopher Isherwood. MacNiece, Isherwood, and Auden had collaborated on literary works in England, and now played ex-patriates together in New York.

Though it was Davis's house in name, Auden played the father role to the bohemian group. The well-known British poet had recently reconverted to Christianity, and was coming to terms with his homosexuality. The war in his homeland left him with guilt over leaving England in her time of need. Auden wrote nothing while in Brooklyn Heights, and decided to move to spur his muse. In the fall of 1941, Auden left New York to teach at the University of Michigan. When he left, the group disbanded. This caliber of writer lived with Lee while she wrote her book, *The G-String Murders*.

Christopher Isherwood lived on Middagh Street in residence in Brooklyn during the same period. Having recently emigrated from England, Isherwood also found himself in a period of guilt over leaving his native land for the less war-torn United States. Although he wasn't writing at the time, Isherwood's work has a 'what-if' quality that mirrors the Lee novel, "What if Gypsy Rose Lee was involved in a murder?" Isherwood moved on after 1941, but he remained one of the few authors who kept in contact with Lee after her stint at the Davis house.

Ironically, George Davis, Lee's landlord, would later claim authorship of the Lee novels, a claim Lee refuted. In mystery circles, bibliographers generally assumed that Craig Rice penned *The G-String Murders* and the novels are listed in Rice's canon; however, for some time literary reviewers have reported that Davis wrote the novel. A number of Auden biographies mention Davis, Lee, and the rumor that he ghostwrote her books, sometimes stated as fact. The mystery remains unanswered. Rice claimed credit for writing the book, but mentions spending a summer with Lee that could never have happened in the frenetic days of 1940. Another doubt niggles. Would writers of the caliber of an Auden or Isherwood tolerate a phony or a ghostwritten book in their presence? Probably not. Auden was known to enjoy a mystery novel, and over the course of his career befriended such genre luminaries as Ken Millar (who wrote as Ross Macdonald) and Margaret Millar. "For me, as for many others, the reading of detective stories is an addiction like tobacco or alcohol."[16] Even with this confession, Auden took the highbrow view in his essay, "The Guilty Vicarage," that mysteries are not art; they represent a pleasant way to pass the time and nothing more. Yet even with his knowledge of literature, Auden takes the narrow viewpoint that detective stories can only be classified as "whodunits," and are not like works by Dickens or Kafka.

With this attitude, some of the premier figures in twentieth century literature would not take kindly to a woman who only *pretended* to write. While the two mysteries cannot be substantiated as coming from Lee's own pen, other sources can attest to her writing skills. Her son, Erik, remembers his mother working on her autobiography, and knows she completed that book without the assistance of others. Her autobiography was successful enough to later become the musical, *Gypsy*.

In addition to her memoirs, Lee also wrote a play called *The Naked Genius*. Mike Todd, the director, (who had brought Lee to Chicago) asked Lee to do the rewrites away from the set, as he was wooing Joan Blondell during the filming. He didn't want his current writer and lover to know about her replacement. Todd vouched for her writing in those days. Lee is reported to have said, "I write my own books and catch my own fish and Erik is really my son." While Lee might have written the book, correspondence reveals that her famous friends helped with ideas for the book, and the revisions. Letters from Lee to Lee Wright at Simon and Schuster indicate significant rewrites were required from the first-time author. A number of these letters were packaged and printed as publicity to quell the rumors that someone else had written *G-String*. In a letter to Lee Wright, she says, "Thanks for the long letter; I got so excited about your suggestions that I bought me a new typewriter. They told me small type was more dignified . . . [W]hen I was in burlesque not one [agent] wanted a piece of me. When I got the Hollywood contract-and I do mean when I got it-they all sued. In the four years they've handled me they haven't gotten me as much as an Elks smoker! NOT ONE DATE!" [17]

The rumors of the authorship ran rampant just before the book's publication, and Simon & Schuster sent out publicity kits with writing samples of Lee's work to squelch the stories. Ironically, one of the letters in the press kit fueled speculation, as it mentioned Rice's novel, *The Wrong Murder*.

If Rice had written the novel, *G-String* would be the only novel in which the protagonist was not an orphan or abandoned by her mother at an early age. While part of Lee's mythology is the character of the pushy mother, the matriarch does not appear in Lee's first mystery. In addition, Rice had no qualms about sounding the publicity horn regarding her involvement in ghostwriting; yet she never bragged about her role in writing the Lee novels except in the interview with *Time* magazine.

A selection from *G-String* details the burlesque house that Lee played in when she came to New York. "The Old Opera wasn't exactly the show place that Moss had affectionately called it, but it was one of the choice burlesque theaters. In the nineties, when only opera was performed there, it must have been considered elegance personified.

"The facade was gray marble, the lobby long and spacious. To the right, there was a wide staircase that led to the balcony and loges. The red carpeting was frayed and worn, the gold leaf peeling symbolically enough from the cherubs that decorated the ceiling. In places, the marble had cracked and been repaired clumsily with plaster . . . The one [picture] of me, wearing a sunbonnet and holding a bouquet of flowers just large enough to bring in the customers and keep the police out, was third from the left."[18]

As proof of Lee's involvement with the novel, some descriptions and scenes from her memoirs evoke the same feelings as the Old Opera theater used in the mystery. This selection from Lee describes a similar place. "From the platform outside our dressing-room door Mother and I could watch most of the show. The wings and the lights hid part of the full stage sets, but we could still see how elaborate they were . . . It was a small stage; the Republic had been a legitimate theatre until Billy Minsky took it over and there wasn't room for the productions he staged. The scenery was stacked against the walls and the prop room was loaded . . ."[19] The level of detail used to describe the people of the theater and the locations themselves would have required Lee to have incredible input into *G-String*, if she did not write the book herself. In addition, the two selections show stylistic qualities that make the reader wonder if both books didn't come from the same hand.

Regardless of who wrote it, *G-String* hit the best sellers list immediately. Sales topped thirty thousand copies in hardback, a number not matched by the leading mystery authors of the day. Craig Rice hardbacks usually sold between fifteen and twenty thousand copies. The book went on to be one of the top sellers of the decade.

The protagonist is none other than Lee herself, writing in first person. H.I. Moss, the owner of a 42nd Street burlesque theater in New York, brings Lee in for a run at the Old Opera. Almost immediately, corpses start piling up, strangled by G-strings. Lee's boyfriend, Biff, solves the case by using her as bait for the killer. Lee used then-boyfriend Mike Todd as the model for Biff, and long-time friend Georgia Sothern as Gee Gee.

The book's background easily comprises the most interesting part of the book. Theater in all its forms has always been an interesting backdrop for mystery. Lee followed a long line of writers, including Ngaio Marsh, Ellery Queen, Patrick Quentin, and Margery Allingham when she used a theatrical setting; however, Lee's novel was the first to show the burlesque theater, not legitimate stage drama. The book contains an almost complete set of burlesque performers, including strippers, a straight man, a tenor, and comics. The hectic four-shows-a-day life draws a vivid picture of life in the theater, and Lee's penchant for rye would make people remember that other famous Chicago writer, Craig Rice.

At the same time, though, the number of characters in *The G-String Murders* makes the introductions confusing. Characters step into the limelight without description or explanation. They have a habit of chiming in during the course of the dialogue with no hint of their function or role in the book or theater. While very enjoyable, *G-String* doesn't reach to an Auden/Davis level. The book contains a double solution that stretches the imagination. As Jack Ketch remarked in his review, the book is "stuff that's worth the price of admission — if you don't shock easy."[20]

In addition to the claims that Rice and Davis wrote the novel, many years later another woman sued Lee, claiming authorship. The case was settled out of court, and no records can be found as to the outcome, but with so many people claiming responsibility for the novel it seems most likely that Lee wrote it herself. The probable scenario is that no one believed that the world's most famous stripper could put pen to paper, and people took advantage of that notion.

CHAPTER F I V E

"Michael Venning's biography has been called for by Who's Who and (for a gag) she has posed for his picture wearing a crepe beard, and her husband's coat."

In early 1942, Rice made good on her promise to move to Los Angeles. Although she had encouraged Nan to take the girls and go there immediately following Elton Rice's death, a year passed before she made the move with third husband, Larry Lipton.

Rice found herself with several reasons to make Los Angeles her new home. With the start of World War II, Rice worried about the fate of her family on the West Coast. The attack on Pearl Harbor left many people skittish about the vulnerability of America's shores. The country had been attacked for the first time since the War of 1812, and the Japanese air strike left everyone apprehensive. Californians especially waited for the inevitable Japanese attack. After her move, one of Rice's first homes was a beachfront property. There were enforced nightly blackouts to protect against the impending Japanese air strikes.

Lipton had wanted the move as well. For a radical, he had traditional ideas about how a family should behave. He felt his family should all live under one roof (except for his own son David from a previous marriage). He arranged to have Rice's children collected in the same household. To this end, ten-year-old David came to California from Wisconsin later in 1942. He remembers the trip well, having traveled on a train from Kenosha to Chicago, and then taking the Super Chief across the United States. The journey took three days, and the train was packed with soldiers heading to the West Coast to protect America's vulnerable shores and replenish the lives lost at Pearl Harbor.

Lipton's brother, David Lipton, had earlier moved to California to work with the motion picture industry. He enticed the couple to Los Angeles with stories of Hollywood and scriptwriting. Some of the best pictures ever made were being produced in Hollywood at this time. *Gone With the Wind*, *Rebecca*, and *The Wizard of Oz* had dazzled audiences two years before, and the film industry bubbled with excitement and money.

The Liptons chose Santa Monica as their home. Just northwest of L.A., Santa Monica was a distinct city in 1941, rather than a suburb of Los Angeles. The distance was made more sizable by the fact that the Liptons didn't drive. Rice had never learned, and the family did not have a car. Rice enjoyed the peaceful seaside town, and made it her home for almost ten years.

The first months in their new home weren't peaceful. Lipton wound up in the hospital shortly after his arrival in Los Angeles, suffering from stomach problems. Despite his rather overbearing nature, he tended to have an anxious disposition. The doctors restricted him to a special diet, about which Rice complained bitterly. By this time, she was writing two books and promoting a third, and wanted to spend her time on her work. Husbands were more disposable.

When Rice contacted Hollywood, one of her first assignments was working on a 'B' picture called *The Falcon's Brother*.

The movie paved the way for George Sanders to leave the *Falcon* series to pursue other film projects. Like Rice, the actor wanted to try everything in life once, and didn't stick with any project for long. Sanders' real-life brother, Tom Conway, took over the series, playing the on-screen brother of the Falcon. In the 1940s, George Sanders played hero roles, The Saint and the Falcon among them. In his heyday, he had choice of plum roles. Many years would pass before he would be cast in more venal parts like the acerbic critic in *All About Eve* his or the voice of Shere Khan, the tiger in Disney's *The Jungle Book*.

Working on the script, Rice teamed with scriptwriter and mystery author, Stuart Palmer. Peas in a pod, the pair hit it off immediately. They drank, laughed a lot, and came up with preposterous movie plots. Palmer had created amateur sleuth Hildegarde Withers, a horse-faced schoolmistress that he had quickly tired of. Like Rice, Palmer had gone through a multitude of careers and spouses before settling down in Hollywood to write mysteries. Palmer had been a taxi driver, newspaper reporter, publicity man, and a clown for Ringling Brothers and Barnum & Bailey. He drank and laughed as much as his partner. The two developed a life-long friendship. The writers remembered those days so fondly that one can believe that not much work was completed on the script as the pair developed their relationship.

Palmer had worked a number of the *Falcon* scripts and had experience with some of the old-time series pictures, including film screenplays for heroes Bulldog Drummond and The Lone Wolf. As the senior writer on the script, Palmer taught Rice the ropes. They became such good friends that on the next *Falcon* picture that Palmer scripted, he included an evil character named Mrs. Lipton. In 1943, Rice worked on another picture in the same series, *The Falcon in Danger*, in which she vowed to get even by naming the villain Palmer. She didn't work with Palmer on this film, probably because of the shenanigans from their last picture together.

Rice employed a new agent when she hit the West Coast. The A. George Volck Agency agreed to market Rice, trying to interest the Hollywood studios in her work. The Ann Watkins agency already represented Rice with the New York publishers, and tried to keep their tempestuous client under control and on a budget. Not an easy task. She frequently asked Ann Watkins for money against the advances and royalties from Lee Wright at Simon & Schuster. Fancy homes, needless luxuries (like an office and secretary for Lipton), and a growing penchant for alcohol cost Rice most of her cash.

Rice's first book in 1942 was *The Big Midget Murders*, featuring one of the most vindictive "orphans" in the Rice canon. Jay Otto, the big midget of the title, grew up knowing that his parents couldn't stand the embarrassment of their diminutive son. The family placed a higher regard on their social standing and good family name. Although given a trust fund by his wealthy biological parents, the midget lived with a foster family in the Midwest, similar to David Ferguson's situation-except that the character grew up mean and spiteful. Jay devised a marriage-blackmail scheme to soak the sons of Chicago's elite, exacting a monetary revenge on those like his parents. "He grew up, hating everybody. Because he was a midget, and - other people weren't. By the time he was twenty-one, he was an orphan, and a - very handsome trust fund had been set up for him. The lawyer who informed him about it - didn't tell him who his parents had been. Just that they had left the money to him - and that it would come to him every month . . . He went on the stage. He didn't need to, he had plenty of money. But he wanted to. It was an outlet for his - hate. His imitations - you know. They were cruel as hell."[1]

Jay Otto, the titular midget, is a nightclub act at Jake's new venture, the Casino. He's turns up dead, hung by a dozen pairs of nylons. The Justuses hide him in a bass fiddle case, and the body subsequently disappears. They call on Malone to find the body and the murderer so that the Casino won't be shut down. Along the way, they discover that the midget had been blackmailing a number of people. He'd devised a scheme in which showgirls married wealthy socialites while intoxicated, and then blackmailed the men with the evidence of their marriage.

Big Midget contains several of the same elements in this book as *The Corpse Steps Out*. Jay Otto's body travels around Chicago in a bass fiddle case. No one can keep up with the location of his corpse. When Malone discovers the corpse for a second time, Otto's body is laid out in bed as if he had died peacefully in his sleep. The issue of money is still causing problems for the Justuses. Jake wants to rescue the Casino he won from Mona McLane in *The Right Murder*. Like Joshua Gumbril's blackmail box, Jay's box of papers caused pain to a number of people who all seemed to be involved with the Casino, including the chorus girls who lost the eleven sets of stockings used to hang the midget.

Fortunately, Malone has a lucrative case, receiving cash for his time and an assignment to defend the murderer.

Despite the unique concept, *Big Midget* cannot be rated as one of the best Rice novels. In this sixth Malone book in four years, Rice reached her saturation point. The characters display no new facets of their personalities, and every character seems to talk over the conversation of others, yearning to be heard above the din. One of the longest books written by Rice, the plot is stretched too thin over the 365 pages. Despite the ever-growing pile of bodies, few clues lead Malone to the murder, and the majority of the clues stem from the first crime. Rice admitted later that this book had been inspired by thoughts of how to remove a corpse in a fiddle case, ruling out an average-sized adult and a child as the victim. Rice did toy with the idea of a child victim in plotting *Big Midget* and even went so far as to use the name of a child she had met. Jay Otto was the name of a youngster Rice had met while dining in New York. On one occasion, she spent the evening with the voice and drama teacher Frances Robinson-Duff in her home and met her hostess' nephews, Arthur and Jay Otto. The two young boys didn't dine with the mystery author that night, but the idea for the name stuck in Rice's head.

Another plot twist that appears in *Big Midget* and repeats in subsequent books is the unnecessary lie. Ruth Rawlson, an older actress with a drinking problem, lies to Malone repeatedly for no apparent reason. "Oh my goodness, he couldn't have! Did I say he invited me? I must have been thinking of some other time."[2] This line becomes Rawlson's mantra throughout the book. At other times, events interrupt the couple before Rawlson can lie again. Rice uses this plot device/book lengthener in several of the later Malone books, much to the reader's chagrin. The better books rely more on the comic plot twists than misunderstandings and lies

Shortly after Rice's arrival in Los Angeles, Bosco Craig came out for a visit. For its thirty years in the making, the visit was anti-climatic. He had been released during a prisoner exchange (just before the war) and suffered from terminal throat cancer. Rice and her family, mostly Nan Rice, nursed him during his final days. Rice would later recall to her agent, "When my father was in his last illness, it was Lipton who talked to doctors, and saw to moving him from hospital to hospital... I had my first screen-writing job, and he didn't want anything to jeopardize it. And after my father died, it was Lipton who tended to all the 'arrangements', and who moved my stepmother, Laura Guerite, from one place to another until the right home was found for her."[3] Actually, despite her memories, Rice's adopted mother, Nan, and not Lipton, tended to Bosco Craig in his final days.

Shortly before Craig's death, Nan Rice came home in a rage. Craig had told her in confidence that he was dying without ever having done what he wanted to do in life. He told that to the woman who had cared for his children and grandchildren, while he cavorted around the world as a free spirit. He died on July 30, 1942. Rice had known her father less than five years of her thirty-four year life.

Although Lipton professed to be a writer at this point, Rice's output supported the family. For the first time since their births, all three children lived with their mother as well as Lipton and Nan Rice. Lipton's first novel, a political diatribe, published in 1942 was *Brother The Laugh is Bitter*. The reviews of the work were mediocre at best.

As Rice's popularity increased, and the challenge of the Malone books decreased, she looked for different creative outlets for her writing. She tried screenwriting first, one of the reasons for the move to California. Rice had been involved in some scriptwriting for radio stations in Chicago, but this new industry fascinated her. A second change of pace involved a new mystery series starring Bingo Riggs and Handsome Kuzak. The series' titles followed a format of "The Day of the Week/Month Animal Murders," the first of which was *The Sunday Pigeon Murders*.

The crime-solving duo in these books lived in a world far removed from the upper crust world of Helene Brand. Street photographers who sold quarter prints to the tourists walking in Central Park, Bingo and Handsome lived a hand-to-mouth existence at best, hawking their cameras and clothes to make ends meet. Bingo was an orphaned schemer who clearly has the brains of the team. Handsome, as his name implies, was the good-looking brawn of the pair, with a twist. He had a photographic memory, and years of newspaper experience. Kuzak could recall anything newsworthy that has happened, along with the weather for the day and sales at any New York department stores.

Once again, Rice cast an abandoned child as the hero of the novel, the orphan made good. "Bingo's father, named Hugh Moishe

Riggs (a judicious blending of the family names of both sets of forefathers), had followed his errant paternal parent to the Pennsylvania mines and perished there. The lovely Mary Margaret had placed her year-old infant in the capable hands of the Sisters of Charity and vanished. That was the state of affairs when Uncle Herman became aware of his family responsibilities, though he did nothing about it for another twelve years.

"But Herman Kutz's grocery and confectionery did well, especially during the dark days of the prohibition era, and he was able to salve his conscience from time to time with reasonably large gifts of money to the Sisters." [4] In her description of Bingo, Rice barely bothers to disguise the names of her own parents in this book.

Once again, the hero is an orphan, deserted by the mother and with no father to speak of. "By all the rules, being an unwanted orphan, Bingo should have turned out to be either talented or brilliant and ended up rich, a pride and joy." [5] Although Rice didn't keep track of her mother, Mary Randolph had returned to Chicago at the time, and lived with her sister. Sacha and Mary Randolph had returned to the United States in 1939, having escaped from Europe on the brink of another world war. They purchased a ranch along the Colorado River, in Arizona. The idea was to ease Sacha Randolph's health problems, presumably lung related. Shortly before the start of the United States' involvement in World War II, he died. Mary Randolph decided to visit her sister, Ethel, in Chicago, where she remained until the end of the war. She worked at her sculpture, and seemed oblivious to her daughter's fame.

The Riggs/Kuzak series dealt with crimes of the past and their impact on the present. In *Sunday Pigeon*, Handsome and Bingo notice a man in one of their photographs, S.S. Pigeon, also known as the Sunday Pigeon for his habit of feeding the birds in Central Park each weekend. Pigeon had disappeared nearly seven years ago. His associates needed to wait a few more days for the courts to declare him legally dead, and then they would inherit Pigeon's sizable estate and business concerns. They retrieve the man and bring him to their small apartment under false pretenses.

Bingo and Handsome soon find themselves over their heads, in trouble and debt when Pigeon's business partner is murdered and gangsters take the duo for a ride. Between worrying about paying their rent and providing food for their semi-hostage, the pair manage to stumble over three more dead bodies before coming up with the solution. Rewarded for their efforts, Riggs and Kuzak have no money worries for the short term.

Bingo and Handsome never captured the public's attention the way Malone and the Justuses had. *Sunday Pigeon* received good reviews in several papers. However, unlike the Malone-Justus series, these books were set on a smaller scale, with fewer stakes. The Justuses were always fighting for their freedom and happiness; in most cases, Bingo and Handsome were looking for money. The people in the books were more everyday as well. The socialites and larger-than-life personalities that appear in the Malone-Justus series are missing, replaced by farmers and blue-collar types. Although the book sold reasonably well, and two more books in the series would be published, the readers always preferred the exploits of the Chicago lawyer and his madcap friends.

Rice followed up *Sunday Pigeon* with another non-Malone book. Although she originally wanted to write under the name Rhys Creighton (a play on her own name), she ended up choosing the name of one of her own characters, Daphne Sanders from *The Wrong Murder*. The book was entitled *To Catch a Thief*, although it was not the inspiration for the romantic Hitchcock film starring Grace Kelly and Cary Grant. Because the book has been out of print for some years, many people assume that the book and the movie stem from the same vehicle.

Thief falls in the adventure suspense category, a first for Rice, although several murders occur in the novel. A mysterious Robin Hood-like character steals from seven millionaires who illegally manipulated the stock market for their own benefit, and caused financial hardship for many others. The thief, John Moon, as he calls himself, converts the jewels and art that he steals into cash. Then he returns that money to the people hurt in the stock market swindle, less his ten percent finder's fee. He notifies his victims in advance, signing his name as "N" for nemesis.

During his work, he accidentally abducts Poppy Hymers, a wealthy debutante who is bored with life. Like so many Rice heroines, she has lost her mother due to the sadistic behavior of her father, Renzo Hymers. Poppy rants to Moon, "If he [Renzo] hadn't been so brutally cruel to my mother, she might have lived."[6] The true villain of the novel, Hymers, masterminded the stock deal that left so many people destitute.

Renzo hires Donovan, a private detective, to solve the case, but the detective quickly learns to admire the skill with which Moon operates. The investigation into the thefts stalls when someone murders Hymers' second wife shortly after Moon robs her. The book is divided equally between Donovan and Moon's viewpoints as they both try to solve the murder. Donovan quickly narrows down the list of suspects to three men: John Casalis, who went broke in the crash and disappeared; John Porter, who had ended up in a French insane asylum after the crash; and Wilfred Hume, one of the seven investors who later regretted his actions. Two more murders take place before Moon identifies the killer and his own identity comes to light.

True love doesn't conquer all in *Thief*. Moon and Poppy Hymers part ways at the end of the book. With this ending, Rice paved the way for a sequel. "Back in the stricken house of Hymers, Donovan sat musing. Someday, somewhere, he knew, his path would again cross that of the man who signed himself 'N.'"[7] She intended to juggle multiple series to keep her creative juices flowing, and the money rolling in. Rice's mind liked to keep multiple balls in the air, and multiple series allowed her to do that within the genre.

Rice followed quickly with a third non-Malone book, this time under the pseudonym of Michael Venning, the wife-beating character from *The Right Murder*. *The Man Who Slept All Day* introduced private investigator Melville Fairr. (Some comment must be made about the names of the Rice protagonists. While the two series have little in common, the names of the characters depict a mindset of law and order, Justus being a corruption of justice, and Fairr of fair. While some of the names in the Rice novels border on the bizarre, for example, Allswell Jackson and Daniel von Flanagan, the monikers of the sleuths seem to fit the characters and their motives.)

Rice's literary talents become apparent in contrasting her series; stylistically the Venning novels have little in common with the Malone books. When they were first published, few guessed that the same author wrote both series. The richness of detail and characterization in these novels don't exist in many other works. Only a moderate amount of drinking, and little humor appear in the books. Fairr is a private detective, but Rice holds tight to any personal information about the little man. Fairr is a wallflower detective. He is described as a small gray man who has a desire to stay in the background and absorb information, as people tend to forget he exists and observes. Fairr receives virtually no character development in the series. He belongs to the same school as Christie's Mr. Satterthwaite from *The Mysterious Mr. Quin*, who realizes the solution to a case by not participating in the action.

  The Man Who Slept All Day uses a country house murder motif with an interesting twist. By page eleven, one of the guests discovers the body of George Faulkner, brother of Frank Faulkner, the owner of Ravensmoor, where the novel takes place. However, no one calls the police for the normal investigation. One by one, each of the seven persons at Ravensmoor discovers George's body, and for his or her own reason, remains mum about the killing. "Tiptoeing into that room, closing the door carefully so that there wouldn't be even the faintest shadow of a sound, moving slowly and quietly across the floor to make sure the man in the bed wouldn't wake - and finding that he would never wake. Realizing that moment, that when the truth became known, the personal lives of every member of the house party would be mercilessly investigated. Who else could be suspected?"[8]A black humor emerges in the slips of the tongue and awkward phrases of the guests in their dealings with each other. The book reminds the reader of the later Hitchcock film, *The Trouble With Harry*, as each person enters George's bedroom and tries to make him look as if he were sleeping although a knife protrudes from his chest.

  The novel concentrates less on the solving of the murder than the romantic relationships of the three couples who had been invited to the country estate. In turn, the viewpoint of each character reveals a secret that George had discovered and taunted them with over the weekend. The malicious host threatens his guests with discovery, though no mention is made of monetary blackmail. Each character shares the secret with his or her significant other. In doing so, the pairs reveal the true depth of their feelings for each other. By the denouement, the reader hopes all of these charming couples will be innocent, so that they can go back to New York City happy and in love. Only Fairr and the two Faulkners do not participate in male-female relationships.

  In a matter of a few short minutes at the end of the book, after a second murder takes place, Melville Fairr reveals that George hired him to help play some vicious prank over the weekend. Fairr took the assignment to control the damage done by this warped man. In fact, in all three Venning novels, Melville Fairr reveals that his client was the victim, giving him unlimited control of his investigation. In *Slept All Day*, the investigation seems an addendum to the novel.

As her backlist grew, Rice turned to meeting other L.A. mystery fans. Shortly after their move to California, Rice introduced herself to a man she had corresponded with while living in Chicago. Ned Guymon, a self-made millionaire and celebrated mystery book collector, had been friends with Ben Abramson and Vincent Starett of Chicago. Guymon collected first editions of all types of mysteries, and had been sent a copy of *8 Faces at 3* by Ben Abramson. Guymon boasted one of the largest mystery libraries in the state of California. Howard Haycraft's book, *Murder for Pleasure*, mentioned his voluminous collection. Guymon had written to Rice, complimenting her on the book, and she replied politely. Their correspondence continued, and Rice sent Guymon first editions of her books as they were published. Her inscriptions were cordial, yet very noncommittal and Guymon chided her on this account more than once.

Rice started the friendship playfully, telling Guymon that she wrote under the Venning name and offering him a copy of *The Sunday Pigeon Murders* if he could guess the origin of the pseudonym. With only a few hints from the author, Guymon guessed correctly that the name appeared in *The Right Murder*, won his prize, and began a friendship that lasted many years. Rice had never been a good money manager and she wasted no time in hitting up Guymon for a loan.

Rice produced so much writing at this point that she hired a young refugee student to help with the typing. There seemed to be no end to her energy. Rice wrote constantly in the times when the children attended camp and Lipton tried to find a publisher for his next book. In retrospect, Rice's abnormally prodigious output can be attributed to bi-polarity, frequently called manic-depressive syndrome. Today the condition is easily treatable as a chemical imbalance (using lithium or other drugs), but the medical discoveries that led to successful treatments would not come until years after Rice's death. The disorder manifests itself in cycles of extreme activity followed by depressive (often lethargic) states. Usually, melancholy dominates the disorder, but in Rice's case, the first thirty-odd years of her life seem to have been one long manic episode, without many depressive cycles. More than simply hyperactivity, the mania results in other behaviors as well. An increased dependence on others, and desperation to maintain relationships frequently occurs (especially in those who are not being treated chemically for the condition). Rice's neediness can be tied to her condition. Bi-polarity is often attributed to heredity or stressful family conditions like those suffered by Rice. In most cases, the disorder is triggered by an extremely traumatic event, like Rice's repeated childhood displacements. Daughter Nancy (who became a counselor as an adult) agreed with the belated diagnosis of her mother. Independent sources (Dr. Scott Becker among them) also agreed with the conclusions, based on what is known about Rice.

In a letter to Fred Dannay, Rice recounts a depressive episode, "Lonely — Fred, it's a kind of deep, inner loneliness that has nothing to do with not having people around. There are people around, constantly. . . . There are no people I can talk with and listen to."[9] Despite these lonely periods, Rice wrote constantly, with bursts of great energy that left others in the dust. Bi-polarity has been linked to the kinds of chemically addictive behavior that Rice suffered from. Her grandiose plans and desire to live beyond her means can also be partially attributed to the disease.

Rice produced the second Michael Venning book in 1943, *Murder Through the Looking Glass*. Again, Melville Fairr appears as the little gray sleuth who blends into the shadows of the case. Rice gives no more information about the detective, other than revealing that he lives alone in a New York City apartment with his cat, Mr. Thomas. The book is almost entirely devoted to the exploits of Jeffrey Bruno, a writer who finds himself falsely accused of murder under another name. A man with Jeffrey's face and the name of his long-dead cousin wakes up on a train. Bruno finds himself accused of killing millionaire Rufus Carrington in his Manhattan home. John Blake, the Bruno alter ego, was an employee of Carrington's grandson and stood accused of embezzling from the firm. Blake had recently proposed to Susan Williams, another Carrington grandchild. "Jeffrey Bruno might have enjoyed it himself, if he hadn't been puzzled. There was the same feeling he had when Susan Williams first looked at him and turned pale. Anyone would be alarmed, to say the least, at seeing the man sought for the murder of one's grandfather standing in the doorway, with a gun in his hand. But not this much frightened. It wasn't a fear that a hunted murderer would kill again in order to escape, or to accomplish some other purpose. It was a fear of something else, and Jeffrey couldn't even guess what it was."[10]

Bruno wakes up on a train to Philadelphia with Mr. Fairr, and reads the newspaper headlines. Unbelieving, the accused man goes back to New York in order to clear his name and learn about the blackouts he has been suffering. Rice's interest in psychology arises again. In an early mystery dealing with multiple personality disorder, Rice weaves a case where the accused and the killer could be the same person, but with different personas. A Dr. Jeckyl and Mr. Hyde scenario in the realm of psychology.

A typical Venning novel contains multiple viewpoints of the suspects, allowing the reader to understand and enjoy each personality. The characterization for each member of the Carrington family is explored in depths rare for mysteries of that era. Fairr doesn't question the characters; instead, the characters examine the reasons for their lives without prodding. The Fairr series uses shifting viewpoints and in-depth characterizations to solve the case. Particularly interesting in this novel is the character of James Carrington, an alcoholic marginally trying to battle his demons. "He'd known for fifteen years that he drank too much and for ten years he'd been trying to stop. It wasn't because of fear or anxiety or worry. It was because he liked everybody, because he liked having a good time."[11] Rice explained her own drinking with similar descriptions. Carrington also shared a Grandmother Church with the author, who grew bolder about adding the names of real people to her books.

While the book is more thriller than straight mystery, Rice does an excellent job of handling the suspense and the element of the police chase in New York. The suspense remains well drawn and palpable throughout *Looking Glass*. However, the readers can determine the killer by realizing that a romantic predicament exists, and that only one solution to that problem remains. Despite that single flaw, *Looking Glass* stands as one of Rice's better novels.

The next Malone and Justuses book was *Having Wonderful Crime*, published in 1944. Like its very successful predecessor, *Trial By Fury*, this book takes place out of the familiar Chicago environs. Jake decides to sell a novel to a New York publisher, and doesn't tell Helene about his quest. While out drinking in the city that never sleeps, they come upon nervous bridegroom Dennis Morrison. The partiers later discover that Dennis' new wife, Bertha Lutts Morrison, has been murdered, or so they think. The headless corpse of a beautiful woman straddles the bed in the Morrison suite, and there is no sign of Bertha. The Justuses, along with their traveling companion, Malone, vow to help their new-found friend. Along the way, Malone meets a woman, Helene gets her poetry published in a literary magazine, and the trio learns the truth about a particularly grizzly murder.

Rice fills *Wonderful Crime* with inside jokes of the New York publishing world. In Jake's latest version of his novel, *The Mongoose Murders*, he contacts the giants in the mystery world of the 1940s. The tongue-in-cheek approach works well at poking gentle fun at the very people Rice dealt with on a daily basis. Editors and trends in publishing received jibes. Rice includes a rejection letter from her editor, Lee Wright of Simon & Schuster. In another twist, outside of the book, Rice had indicated via letters to her agent that her next Bingo and Handsome book would be entitled *The Monday Mongoose Murders*. A typical Rician touch tied the series together this way.

The author also poked fun at the literary types she had known over the years. Helene decides to write poetry by using the fad of picking words from a hat. Rice inserts several snippets of her poetry into the novel, passing them off as the work of character Wildavine Williams. The head of Zabel publishing decides to publish Helene's work on a whim, defying all the rules of hard work and perseverance in writing.

Despite all the jokes and the New York atmosphere, *Wonderful Crime* has internal problems. The plot, compelling but thin, devotes too much time to Jake keeping Helene in the dark about his book without good reason. Helene had never shown a snobbishness or disdain for writers (or anyone) in the past, having supported all of Jake's careers. Additionally, Jake spends too many pages hiding from the cops. Rice also uses a plot device that doesn't really work in this novel. She would use it again in *The Lucky Stiff* with more success. The characters in this book want a quick buck, and the reader cannot sympathize with their plight.

One of the more interesting aspects of the novel is Rice's open reference to homosexuality. The previous year Marie Rodell, at that time editor at William Morrow, had written a book entitled *Mystery Fiction: Theory and Technique*. She stated in the book, "Homosexuality may be hinted at, but never used as an overt and important factor in the story. An author may, in other words, get away with describing a character in such a fashion that the reader may conclude the character is a homosexual, but he should not so label him."[12] Rice challenged that taboo in *Wonderful Crime*, and went one further. Bertha Lutts Morrison is described as an unattractive woman, but also "Bertha liked girls, not boys . . . She got this young man to marry her . . . so people wouldn't talk. Because they were talking, a little. I don't know where she found him. He was a professional dancing partner or something. I do know she hired him to marry her. They were going to go on a big honeymoon tour."[13] The character's sexual preference crops up as a motive for murder. While her characters rely on stereotypes of gays, Rice enjoyed turning mystery's clichés on their ear, and also tried to expand the form to include ideas that had not been used before. Unlike many of the other ideas and social issues that Rice experimented with, there is no indication that Rice met or knew any gays or lesbians in the relevant time period.

Rice had not one but two homosexuals in this book, and neither of them could be considered model citizens (one a blackmailer, the other an escort). In 1944, gays and lesbians were not a popular topic with the reading public. Despite expanding the genre with her characters, Rice chose to portray the characters as victims and villains, not as hero or heroine. Mystery fiction did not cover homosexuality; it appeared only in underground works or in less than straightforward presentations. Only a few mainstream references had been made to homosexuality. In *The Maltese Falcon*, Joel Cairo and the boy Wilmer received the contempt of most of the other characters for their sexual preference. Four years after *Wonderful Crime*, in *A Murder is Announced*, Agatha Christie's Heathcliff and Murgatroyd come to mind as a possible lesbian couple living together, although there is no overt reference to the fact, much as Rodell had stated in her book.

Rice's next project fell outside the mystery genre entirely. Although she had fame and fortune by this point, Rice honestly believed Lipton to be the better writer in the family. Lipton looked down upon the mystery novels that Rice produced, even though the royalties paid his bills. Rice fell victim to that same snobbery to some degree. To remedy this situation and gain Lipton's approval, she decided to write serious novels that dealt with themes outside of the mystery field. Despite her best efforts, years later Lipton would claim to be the sounding board for all Rice's mystery plots. Later still, he would profess co-authorship. Despite these claims, Lipton felt himself a literary writer, worthy of some notice.

To this end, Rice wrote *Telefair*, a book dealing with what she called "inward reality" or the dream state. "In *Telefair* it's not the things that happen which are important but the things that seem to happen . . .. perilously balancing the narrative between the real world of the tangible and physical and the dream world of the mind, the seeming world."[14] Usually when something needs to be explained in such detail, the concept isn't worth understanding and this novel proved no exception.

Telefair tells the story of David Telefair, whose Uncle Philip requests him to come to Telefair Island. Another orphan, David's parents died shortly after his birth. An uncle he has never met has supported him. Like Rice's son, this fictional David has lived a life of upheaval, moving from boarding school to boarding school. He has developed no sense of home over the years. When he arrives on the island, his cousin, Edris, and one of the housekeepers quickly warn him of the danger of this place and that he should leave immediately. The novel unfolds at a snail's pace until the last few pages. The meaning of the veiled warnings and the true fate of David's parents are explained.

> .".He had left the house behind him, so perfectly
> hidden from sight that he wondered, indeed, if he would
> ever find it again. Behind him he could only see a
> rolling, shifting wall of mist; ahead of him, where the
> gardens were, there was a veritable sea of fog, more white
> than gray, filmy and translucent before his face, pale and
> impenetrable a little beyond."[15]

These descriptions go on for pages with little action, dialogue or movement. Paragraphs and chapters are devoted to detailed descriptions of the mood and scene. The book can best be described as a Gothic romance, relying more on the atmosphere of Telefair Island and the mansion than plot or action. At one point late in the novel the reader discovers that a great deal of what has supposedly transpired was a dream, and the realization leaves the reader feeling cheated.

Rice wrote fast-paced, humorous mystery stories. Few writers, excepting authors like Joyce Porter, Edmund Crispin, Taylor McCafferty, and Joan Hess have been able to come close to her in writing comic mysteries. Most authors settle for an occasional chuckle, and don't go for the belly laugh. A slowly paced Gothic novel with never-ending descriptions of dusk, dawn, and fog takes a different set of writing skills, which Rice didn't have. Her attempts to do something with more psychological impact come together better in the Venning books, which have an atmosphere of intrigue, but also have a substantial plot. Sadly, the Gargoyle label, a short-lived line of mysteries from Coward-McCann, published the Venning books. They cannot be readily found today.

Rice had originally planned to make *Telefair* part of a trilogy dealing with the "inward reality" concept. The second book of the trio Rice tentatively titled *The Days of Wine and Roses* (no connection to the award-winning movie). The book followed the adventures of Emily du Perrierre, following her life as she grew old and died. Rice intended the book as a metaphor of Europe and America, with Emily representing the older society and her children as the heirs to civilization in the New World. Rice wrote part of the book on more than one occasion; never satisfied with the results, she trashed most of the novel every time she read it.

Rice planned to call the final book in the series *Martin Faville*. Martin, a man in poor health, is saved by his distant cousins, who run a home for mentally-challenged young women. Rice planned the book as a contrast of good and evil, visually presented as black and white. John and Margaret, the cousins, were to be presented as "the 'holy good'," as Rice referred to it, people unaffected by the evil or trouble in their environment. Martin falls in love with a cousin who had been killed in a train wreck. The reader finds out that the beloved cousin is just a memory, kept alive by the people at the convent. A good section of the book simply recapped past events so that the reader would understand what had happened. Rice never wrote this book, and nothing can be found of *Faville* other than a partial synopsis.

MGM picked up an option on *Wonderful Crime* in 1943 and Rice received a check for $7,250 for the rights to the book. Although the

Volck agency had shopped all of her books to the various producers, this marked the first serious interest shown in a Rice work by the Hollywood studio system.

Hollywood had shown great interest in filming *G-String*, which led to Gypsy Rose Lee publishing a second mystery, *Mother Finds A Body*. While Rice did not write *G-String*, rumors swirled that she had written the second book for Lee. *Time* magazine reported that Rice wrote the second Gypsy Rose Lee novel while she was living with Lee "one summer in Connecticut"[16]; however, notes from the interview could not corroborate that point. Given the factual lapses in the rest of the interview, most likely Rice misstated her involvement in the book. The timing of the book remains a question because the summer in question would logically be the summer of 1942, since *Mother* relies on plot points from *G-String*. Yet Rice was very involved with her first Hollywood assignments and her father's death at that same time. And in this case, Rice had confirmed the rumors of authorship; however, like many of her other claims, there doesn't seem to be any basis or proof for those stories. No contracts exist. No notes exist from Lee Wright to Rice. No mention of the book in the letters to her friends. If Rice did ghostwrite *Mother*, she proved no match for the literary assistance of Gypsy's former housemates, and the book failed miserably with the public.

The situation was made worse because the publisher had approved a huge first print run, leaving Simon & Schuster in the lurch. Ironically, with the book that didn't make the bestseller list, no one stepped up to claim it as his or her work (as had been the case with *G-String*). Crushed, Lee did not attempt any more mystery writing. She wouldn't attempt another full-length work until her memoirs, published in the 1950s.

The second novel in the stripper's series removed the single best feature of the first book, the background in burlesque, and replaced it with a trailer park in a small Texas town. While mystery might have a long love of the theater, there is no tradition between mystery and trailer parks. Biff and Gypsy have just married and begun a trek across country with a full trailer of guests including Evangie, Gypsy's mother. The tension and animosity between mother and daughter cuts through the dialogue. Rice could have written their scenes from her life.

"[T]he trailer camp settled down to sleep again. The smell of burnt brush and chemicals coming from the woods was like a badly kept Turkish bath, but my nose had been subjected to such a variety of odors during the last week that it was losing its sensitivity. Anyway, I kept it close to the pot of coffee that was boiling away on the relief stove, so the smell didn't bother me. . ."[17] Scenes like this make *Mother* less exciting and more like a travelogue of a bad vacation.

Many of the characters from the first book appear in *Mother Finds a Body*, including friends Gee Gee, Mandy, Joyce Janice, (Biff's old girlfriend, who happens to show up in the town) and others. Yet, without the unifying background of the theater, the book loses its charm. When a body turns up in the trailer, which had been stashed there before leaving San Diego, Evangie decides to dispose of it illegally and the action begins. Some of the cast find jobs at a local burlesque hall and stumble onto an illegal drug operation. The group begins to suspect each other of the crimes, and the tension grows among the trailer park residents until Gypsy solves the crime.

One of Rice's undisputed own, the second Bingo-Handsome novel, *The Thursday Turkey Murders*, came out in 1943. The book opens with the pair running over a turkey in the town of Thursday, Iowa. Fresh from New York with their reward from *The Sunday Pigeon Murders*, the two buy a turkey farm and move in, hoping for a quick profit. Riggs and Kuzak soon find that they've been swindled, and that the land they "purchased" hides a quarter million in missing gold and some escaped convicts determined to find it. Bingo decides that they should search for the missing loot to make back their losses, and the pair begin their investigation of rural America.

The book is standard Rice fare: hard-hitting, fast and funny. The book depicts the hand-to-mouth existence that Rice had perfected over the years with her constant requests to her agent, and shows the conundrum of con men being conned. Still, the book cannot be counted among her best for two specific reasons. First, because of its small town setting, *Thursday Turkey* must be compared with *Trial By Fury*, one of Rice's best works, with an accurate and insightful picture into small town life. *Thursday Turkey* doesn't transcend the typical mystery farce novels that Rice wrote. Published within two years of the other, better novel, comparisons will crop up. For example, the character of Christine Halvorson remains one-dimensional. She only represents the clichéd farmer's daughter, of whom so many jokes are made. Rice over-plays the situation by having not one, but both of the heroes kiss her in the barn. "For a moment, he forgot the troubles surrounding him, and even the imminent danger, looking at her. This was *really* the farmer's daughter, and no doubt about it. She had on a pink cotton dress and a cute ruffled apron. Her golden blond hair was in pigtails, with little pink bows at the ends. She carried a basket on her arm."[18] Her charac-ter never becomes anything more than a comic sketch.

Secondly, the plot turns on unbelievable points, most noticeably a character in the book that knows the solution throughout the mystery, but doesn't reveal the truth because no one bothered to ask him. While this character provides some humor to the book, the plot device stretches the reader's willingness to suspend disbelief for this unlikely scenario. "I committed no crime. I happened to be present at the scene of one. I was being held in jail as a material witness when the court-house burned down, the sheriff absconded with the county funds, and the judge suffered a stroke and died. . . I was the only witness who could identify all the participants."[19]

Rice's impudent child characters appear in this novel. Rice used her child characters sparingly here as well as in *Home Sweet Homicide* and *Knocked For a Loop*. Her books were more likely to be populated with big kids. Unlike so many novelists whose children act like angels or imbeciles, Rice bestows her children with adult characteristics in small forms. Authors have long found it difficult to accurately portray children as fictional characters. Artie, the leader of the campers, can be amusing and realistic at the same time, despite his penchant for four-letter words (even that trait makes him less artificial). Rice would later perfect her child characters as the alter egos for her own brood in *Home Sweet Homicide*.

Rice made forays into short story writing in 1943 at the urging of her friend, Fred Dannay. Dannay wrote as half of the writing team of Ellery Queen and also published the then fledgling *Ellery Queen's Mystery Magazine*. William A.P. White [Anthony Boucher] had intro-duced them and told Rice of Dannay's offer of $100 for original short stories. For one of the first issues, he encouraged Rice to write a Malone short story. The resulting story, "His Heart Could Break," dis-tinguished Rice as a superior short fiction writer.

"His Heart Could Break" contains the elements that make a good

Rice novel: the impossible plot; the cast of regular characters; and of course, plenty of alcohol. Malone has just won a new trial for his client, Paul Palmer, and goes to visit him in the Statesville Prison. He and the guards find Palmer hung from the ceiling, almost dead. He gasps, "It wouldn't break"[20] before dying and Malone is off to seek vengeance on behalf of his client. Ironically, Dannay, as part of the Ellery Queen writing team, made frequent use of the dying message.

Warden Garrity, a character from the upcoming *The Lucky Stiff*, appears in this story along with Joe the Angel, Max Hook, and Orlo Featherstone. Probably the most different character in the Malone short stories is Malone himself, a more intelligent and sensitive character in the short fiction than in some of the longer works. By now Malone's popularity had soared to a point that he could appear without the Justuses.

Another short story that appeared around the same time was "Dead Men's Shoes" in *Baffling Detective*, a pulp magazine. Bad Luck Bradley, a wealthy philanthropist, tries to help the bums on West Madison in Chicago. His name comes from the fact that the bums he assists, and his own family, seem to be disappearing at a rapid rate. Gerda Powell enlists a willing Malone to find her brother, who lived in one of the West Madison flophouses and can't be found. The trail of the brother leads Malone to Bradley and his family.

Although Rice found the story engaging, the work represented a letdown in Rice's work. The end of the story leaves too many loose ends and the plot stretches the reader's imagination. With the amount of writing that Rice produced in this period, some ideas couldn't translate into a cohesive work.

CHAPTER S I X

"In 1944 Craig Rice wrote a book, Home, Sweet Homicide, in which liquor was not even mentioned."

Rice's prodigious output of 1942-43 gave her a revered spot in the mystery field as one of its rising stars. That standing allowed Rice to return to literary criticism, one of her early loves. Harking back to the days when she had critiqued radio shows for midwestern magazines, Rice now went after the mystery novel. She wrote a bi-weekly column for *The Chicago Daily News* entitled, "It's a Mystery To Me." The column debuted July 7th, 1943 and gave Rice a wide berth to measure the current output of books.

"Once upon a time my favorite newspaper editor was asked by an unfriendly critic, 'Why do you publish so much crime news in your paper?' His answer was, 'Because there's so much crime.'

"So when David Appel asks me indignantly why I send him so many mystery novel reviews, I shall say, with calm and magnificent dignity, 'Because there are so doggone many mystery novels published.'

"Reviewing mystery novels must, of necessity, be more a matter of selection than criticism. Therefore, I shall have to confine myself to those I can honestly recommend."[1]

The column mixed gossip rag with serious criticism to provide insights into mysterydom of the war years. Most of her columns opened with remarks about various authors and pseudonyms, an area that Rice especially enjoyed. Then the reviews of typically two to three books followed. The newspapers provided Rice with scores of advanced review copies of mystery novels, which she promptly sold to Ned Guymon for his collection. Her private reviews to Guymon, a word or two scribbled on the book list, gave more insight and honesty than the column. On several occasions, she labeled books by friends or well-known authors as stinkers.

Publicly, her reviews were much kinder as she only took on books that she could highly recommend. In her review of Margaret Millar's novel, *Fire Will Freeze*, Rice reports, "The bus driver walks out into a Quebec snowstorm and disappears, leaving stranded a load of passengers none of them ordinary and some of them slightly mad. When the passengers finally make their way to an eerie and probably haunted mansion, they are met by rifle bullets, a charming, elderly, female lunatic, and a very grim nurse companion. Then follows the incident of the cat and I dare you to stop reading beyond that point. Hilarious!"[2] Rice's reviews delivered superficial accounts of the books that tried not to give away the ending to the reader.

Of Phyllis Whitney's *Red is for Murder*, Rice wrote, "this magnificently plotted story in which the first murder takes place in a State Street department show window. A big department store is the setting and the atmosphere is so interesting (and so well described) that it would be well worth reading even if it didn't include an exciting murder mystery."[3] As a reviewer, she could get excited for other people's works and highly recommend them if she felt the book deserving. Yet in the insular world of mystery fiction in the 1940's, she often reviewed the work of close friends.

Rice met and became friends with another mystery reviewer in California, William A.P. White, better known as mystery author Anthony Boucher. Boucher (who wrote mystery fiction under the Boucher name as well as H.H. Holmes) started reviewing for *The San*

Francisco Chronicle and would later write for *The New York Times* as a mystery columnist. He was perhaps the most respected mystery reviewer in the history of the genre. He and Rice frequently met at Rice's house in Santa Monica to discuss the trends and rising stars of the mystery field, along with author Dorothy B. Hughes, who also reviewed mysteries. Hughes would later recall, "He (Tony Boucher) always came to Rice's and we'd meet up there, sit on the broad steps and talk of the books we'd reviewed. This in the long summer afternoons. Rice with her drink, Tony and I with cokes. Mystery writers then as now always talk of mystery books."[4] Ironically, Hughes reviewed Rice's books for *The Chicago Daily News.*

As noted by Dorothy B. Hughes, Rice's drinking became more open and more frequent after her move to California. In Fort Atkinson and Chicago, she had kept her drinking limited to social events and, surreptitiously, at home. As Rice met more people in the Santa Monica area, she and Lipton began to have regular Sunday parties for their friends. The parties gathered large numbers of writers, discussing their books and consuming lots of liquor. Francis Towner Laney, the well-known science fiction fantasy fan, recalled, "I never saw anyone get out of line there, but on the other hand the amount of booze flowing around the place made it really rugged for me, since I was supposed to be working regular hours, while few of the others were. These parties used liquor in the way I've always felt the stuff was designed to be used: as an ice-breaker and tongue-loosener; and such was the high level of most of the conversation that partaking in it burned up most of the alcohol as fast as it was drunk."[5]

These Sunday parties left the hosts extremely hung over on Monday. Nancy remembers finding stacks of bottles outside the window on the morning after a party. As Rice became more open about her drinking (and its increased frequency), her output began to slow and grew sloppy. Alcohol depresses the central nervous system, and Rice began experiencing more and deeper depressive cycles in her bipolar disorder.

In mid-1944, Larry published another book, *In Secret Battle.* Rice asked Boucher to bring the novel to the attention of the reviewers of *The San Francisco Chronicle*. Rice tried to get the book the publicity she felt it deserved as a piece of literary fiction. She still thought of Lipton as the "real" writer in the family, although, with his pretensions, his attitude wore thin at times. The didactic manner he displayed to his family came through in his work.

Boucher's reply cut to the point, "... it was still a bad book... I'm afraid I don't even think ISB is good propaganda in that it demands, rather than seduces agreement from the reader. I have a notion that those who do not in advance agree with the author will be, not converted, but simply infuriated. ... how can such a magnificently humorous conversationalist and raconteur as Larry become so heavyhandedly serious in front of a typewriter?"[6] Lipton's book received little critical attention and sunk from sight.

The tension between the married authors grew worse because Rice's next book was arguably her best. *Home Sweet Homicide*, a semi-autobiographical work, didn't include her usual series characters. Rice presented a charming domestic portrait of the middle 1940s with fudge cakes, two dollar manicures, and carbon papered typing. The book features mystery writer Marian Carstairs, who pumps out four books a year to support herself and her three children, April, Dinah, and Archie. When someone murders their nasty neighbor, Flora Sanford, the children decide to solve the murder and garner the publicity for their mother's career. By far the breeziest and most lighthearted of the Rice canon, at this writing, the book is sadly out of print.

The children were realistically portrayed as adolescents, a difficult task for any writer, much less their own mother. The children question the neighbors, check alibis, confound the police with their stories, and finally uncover the killer. They even foil a wartime spy, and uncover their mother's pre-marriage career as a crime reporter who covered a bizarre kidnapping story. In a bitter twist, April weeps as she unmasks the murderer, telling her mother how she put the clues together to confront the friendly killer. "'Oh,' said April, 'oh, no!' She turned white. It must be true, but I didn't want it to turn out that way.'"[7]

Despite the fact that this was Rice's second entry in the Haycraft-Queen Definitive Library list, *Time* magazine would later criticize this work and report that many magazines had turned down the opportunity to serialize the novel "because the children showed an impish disrespect for the police."[8] The children hampered the police at every turn, giving an alibi to their neighbor who was the prime suspect, and confounding the officers. Only when the three try to fix their mother up with Lieutenant Bill Smith do they manage to be respectful.

One of the more interesting items in the book is the description of Rice's writing style. "From upstairs in the big old stucco house they could hear the faint purr of a typewriter, working at top speed. Marian Carstairs, alias Clark Camerson, alias Andrew Thorpe, alias J.J. Lane, was finishing another mystery novel. When it was done, she would take a day off to have her hair shampooed and to buy presents for the young Carstairs. She would take them extravagantly out to dinner and to the best show in town. Then the next morning she would begin writing another mystery novel."[9] The manic quality to her writing becomes apparent in the novel. Angry after a fight with Bill Smith over what she knows about the kidnapping, Marian storms upstairs without notes or plot to begin a new mystery, and spends most of the night working on it. "They listened and heard the unmistakable sounds of paper being inserted in a typewriter. It was followed by a sudden fury of typing. Then a paper was ripped out and thrown away, and another inserted. The typing began again, still furious. This time, it kept on. . . Mother was sitting at the desk, still in the blue house coat, her back hair coming down, and her eyes blazing. The kittens were sitting bolt upright on the desk, looking interested and slightly alarmed."[10] In some ways so real to life, Rice's cats even make it into the novel, chewing on the manuscripts and leaving paw prints much like those on the copies donated to the Occidental College library in Los Angeles by Ned Guymon.

While the novel resembles Rice's life at a superficial level, the similarity stops there. Jerry Carstairs, the father of the three precocious children, bears a faint resemblance to Bertie Ferguson. The journalist father traveled extensively and died just before the publication of Marian's first book. However, Marian was only married once, and alcohol doesn't appear in *Home Sweet Homicide*. Rice's own children had only spent a few years with her and attended boarding schools by the time the book published. In fact, between Rice's writing and drinking, she found little time to manage the children and left the details of the household up to Lipton, who ran the house like a prison camp.

Rice spent most of 1944 trying to find a producer for *Home Sweet Homicide*. With her working for the movies, the family had become infected with the film bug. Shortly before the release of the book, the property passed through many of the big Hollywood film companies. Donald Friende of A&S Lyons, Rice's new West Coast agent, had replaced Bill Schiffrin at the Volck Agency. Rice felt that Schiffrin hadn't done much with her properties, except get them tied up with RKO. The studio repeatedly optioned the Malone series, but never produced a film. Rice later discovered several of the plots had been cannibalized into other films for other detective series, rendering the options and the mysteries useless for film.

Unfortunately, no one optioned *Home Sweet Homicide* immediately. Rice found herself wooed by several major producers, but at Rice's insistence, the asking price for the property remained $50,000, a huge figure for that day. "Stromberg plied me with rich and rare foods, tried to find out how much the price of *HSH* was going to be, gave me a big sales talk about what a wonderful picture he could make from it, and wants to confer with me on Sunday. Gypsy [Rose Lee] phoned and asked me to lunch in her dressing room on the Belle of the Yukon set; turns out it's because Otto Preminger has a burning yen to meet me, and he spends the afternoon selling himself to me as just the right man to do *HSH* with Claudette Colbert as Marian Carstairs; drove me home..."[11] Rice felt ambivalent about giving her domestic, well-written mystery to the studios to ruin. Too many times she'd seen Hollywood strip a book of its originality to get to the screen. Theater options for the book were available in New York, and Rice leaned towards doing the play.

Finally, Rice decided to go with a movie option for a much lower asking price of $20,000. Her financial difficulties settled the decision to go with the movies. Rice continued to spend money faster than she could earn it, and the lure of cash from Hollywood made her decide on a film. Margot Johnson of the Ann Watkins Agency spent most of her time trying to collect royalties from the publishers for her famous client's infamous needs.

Rice continued to get advances against books that would not be written and slowly eroded her credibility. By the end of 1944, she owed three books to three separate publishers, only one of which would ever see print. When *Jethro Hammer* came out, the novel received press as a psychological thriller — not as a straight mystery. Rice thrilled at the crossover, but the notice caused problems with Bobbs-Merrill, the publisher of *Telefair*. They had signed a contract with Rice for first option on any book in a similar vein as *Telefair*, the "inward reality" concept she'd touted just two years before. Rice's novels under the Venning name approached a fine line where her old contract could be applied, and Bobbs-Merrill approached the agency about the book. The next book for Bobbs-Merrill Rice had titled *The Days of Wine and Roses*, very similar to a planned fourth installment in the Fairr series, *The Trouble with Roses*. Rice never finished the fourth Fairr novel, although she spent the advances.

Rice wrote one book that went to the publisher but never hit the presses. *The Countess*, as she referred to the novel, featured Jake and Helene without the assistance of Malone. Rice had been leaning towards Malone as the main character, (especially in her short fiction) and this marked a departure for her. Rice sent the novel to Simon & Schuster, only to find that Dorothy Hughes had sent in a novel with almost the identical plot. Rice was devastated because they had not discussed their work as friends or reviewers and the work was rendered useless, although Lee Wright had already given Rice most of the advance. Sadly, the book introduced Helene Brand Justus' mother, a character missing from *The Wrong Murder*. If she resembled her madcap daughter, the loss was truly regrettable. The mix-up took a toll on Rice, who lost some of her confidence in the originality of her ideas. No record exists of the manuscript today.

Rice took the time to write a magazine article on the art of writing a mystery for *The Writer* magazine which she entitled, "It's a Mystery to Me", the same as her review column. The article, long on jokes and short on true advice, contains little help for a beginning writer. Her most valuable suggestion is the time honored "put a clean sheet of paper in the typewriter. At the top . . . type page one."[12] Rice admitted that she didn't know what made a good mystery and neither did any of her friends. In fact, during discussions at one of Rice's parties, they "hadn't even agreed on what was a successful mystery novel."[13] Considering the amounts of alcohol consumed at one of these parties, a lively disagreement could have been expected.

Besides her novels and the occasional article, scriptwriting continued to bring in money as Rice worked on *The Eddie Cantor Story*, writing a treatment of it for RKO. Rice received two thousand dollars to work on the script. The studio permitted her to work on revisions as time permitted so as not to impact her writing schedule. Rice was doing anything at this point in order to bring in money.

However, the studios brought little joy to Rice. She filed a lawsuit against RKO in 1945 for allegedly using material from four of her books that were under option without proper credit or payment. Parts of the Malone books were used in other RKO series films. Many of the Jake-Helene-Malone books had been kept under option by RKO for years, although no Rice films appeared. She felt that the use of the books made them unsalable. She sued for $14,000 and a release from the option contract. RKO chose not to settle and went to court over the matter. That decision postponed any money that she might have expected.

While Rice's fame grew, so did her expenses. Lipton had an office away from home in which to write. On the other hand, Rice worked at home. She had a desk in the corner of one room, next to a dressing table that had mannequin legs to hold up the tabletop and a skirt around it depicting can-can girls. As time (and money) permitted, she hired someone to help out. The longest lasting secretary, Peggy O'Leary, typed and handled her correspondence.

The family continued to move, on a regular basis, to ever-larger homes. The children went to boarding schools. Rice always lived hand to mouth ,and used her friendship with Ned Guymon to make ends meet. The collector frequently received long letters accompanied by books she had reviewed (given to her by The Chicago Daily News). In return, Guymon paid her for the additions to his mystery library.

She always seemed to have a good reason to be broke, with the prospect of money coming in at any moment. "To come right out and say it, can you lend me, fast, $1500 on very good security and at 6% interest, for ninety days?

"In case you're wondering why a successful novelist and a screen writer should be in the position of having $89 in the bank and having to pay some $900 in bills the first of this week — I'll explain. I had counted on a substantial payment from RKO on the release date of *HAVING WONDERFUL CRIME*. The release date has been shoved ahead a month because of a tangle in bookings. Ordinarily, I would have a reserve for just such emergencies. But my working for Warner Brothers for six weeks was a bad financial mistake. Due to the wage ceilings, they could only pay me $250 a week. Deduct my agent's 10%, deduct the witholding (sic) tax, deduct Motion Picture Relief Fund and Social Security, and you can figure out what I got every week. Not only was I unable to lay any of it away but, it didn't meet household expenses during that period. In that period I could have written a book on which I would have received at least a $1500 advance. I knew all that at the time I took the job, but on the other hand, *DANGER SIGNAL* was a 'prestige' writing job and, frankly, I was crazy about the story and wanted to do it."[14] she wrote to Guymon. The millionaire kept the loans on a business basis with collateral and interest, but their personal relationship provided the basis for the monetary assistance.

Despite their frequent calls, letters, and loans, no indication exists that Rice and Guymon had a sexual relationship. Ned appeared happily married with a newborn daughter at the time, and Rice lived with Lipton. Guymon's daughter, Jane, recalls that Ned would light up whenever Rice's name came up in conversation, and that he enjoyed her visits to San Diego.

Due to Rice's lack of willpower in money matters, Lipton took control of the family finances late 1944. He didn't bother to manage within a budget, either. The Liptons' marriage started to show the strain of the constant financial burden. Rice wrote to her agent asking for advances, explaining, "I love Larry terribly, and he loves me ditto, but we came to actual physical combat over this thing. And I actually had to wait until he was out and then go through his room and dig all the little bills he'd simply neglected to pay out of his files."[15] For her faults, Rice managed money better than Lipton, who simply ignored bills that he couldn't pay. This didn't ease Lipton's rage, or his increasingly frequent physical abuse. The children remember intense battles between the Liptons.

In July of 1945, Rice went in to the hospital for minor surgery. She had hoped to push the operation out until money matters improved, but the procedure couldn't wait any longer. Rice, plagued by feminine problems, had to postpone writing. Ever one to tell a good story even while she was down, Rice recounted to friends how Iris had referred to her surgery as work on her 'social system.'

Eye problems continued to plague Rice during this time period also, causing a slowdown in her writing. The interruptions made Rice go weeks without putting finger to keyboard, which exacerbated the money problems. A weak right eye ran in the Rice family, inherited by both Nancy and David. In addition, Rice suffered from glaucoma at an early age, which caused some blurriness in her vision. Over the next decade, Rice would lose all sight in her right eye. When her sight gave out completely in that eye, she made an offer of donating the orb to science to help a sightless person. The media picked up on the story and Rice, in her usual fashion, elaborated on the story to tell about the collection of glass eyes that she wanted to buy.

As her popularity grew, Rice's interests went even further afield. Trying to cash in on her fame, Bond-Charteris Enterprises published the *Craig Rice Mystery Digest* in 1945. Bond-Charteris was a highly respected, small, private press with interests in the mystery field. Leslie Charteris was responsible for the *Saint* series. The pocket book and digest-style magazine had become a publishing phenomenon just after the end of World War II, and Charteris wanted to cash in on it. A single issue published that year contained 4 highly abridged novels, one from Rice (*The Big Midget Murders*, three years old) and one by her good friend, Dorothy Hughes.

The timing for the project couldn't have been worse. Bond and Charteris wanted to divide the corporation, although each would continue publishing separately. Rice enjoyed the fame associated with this project, but didn't put much effort into making a success of the magazine. Her contributions seem to be limited to the single previously published novel and writing numerous letters to show off the digest's stationery with her name across the top in big letters. Unfortunately, Rice counted on the money as a steady source of additional income and adjusted her spending accordingly.

Rice continued writing for the movies as time and money permitted. She was involved with Stromberg's *Queen of Burlesque* picture, which her agents only referred to as a mess. The movie was originally supposed to be the screen adaptation of *The G-String Murders*, but the end product bore little resemblance to the best-selling novel. Barbara Stanwyck starred as Gypsy, renamed Dixie for the film. Although Rice didn't receive a screen credit for the film, her participation only fueled the rumors surrounding her authorship of the Lee books.

The studio called her in to rewrite on the script for *Danger Signal*, a Warner Brothers picture based on Phyllis Bottome's work. Her agents tried to get Rice better assignments, to improve her standing in the motion picture community. She only received $250 a week to write for the movies (on the low side at the time) but her track record hadn't been sterling. Her known output consisted of the *Falcon* pictures and the RKO mess and lawsuit. The agents' goal was to allow Rice enough prestige in the film world to write the screenplays of her own works, giving her more control over the final product.

The film bug bit Rice's daughter, Iris, too. She dropped out of high school in the tenth grade to take acting lessons at the Geller Theater Workshop. When a repertory company asked her to join, she left home to pursue her dream. Glad to leave the abusive Larry Lipton, she went on the road with the Century Theater Group.

The first film adapted from Rice's work came out in 1945. RKO, the same studio Rice had problems with her options under contract filmed *Having Wonderful Crime*. The only things that the novel and movie have in common are Malone, the Justuses and the title. Even Malone has been changed by Hollywood to be Michael J. Malone. Some of the chemistry and banter between the trio exists, and the irrepressible Helene glows no matter what. The plot of Jake writing a mystery novel has been replaced with the death of stage magician who has a check for $50,000. After solving a Chicago murder case, the Justuses head off with for their honeymoon, with Malone unwanted by them and wanted by the police. When Helene runs a young girl off the road with her driving, the foursome head to a lakeside lodge. The lodge houses a pair of batty sisters, an oversized porter, and several shadows at the windows. After a near-death encounter with the killer, Malone wraps up the case for the police. Pat O'Brien stars as Malone, and the Irish actor plays the overworked, rumpled attorney well.

To ensure a good script with her next project, Rice chose to go to work at Twentieth-Century Fox for the treatment of *Home Sweet Homicide*. Fresh from her experiences with *G-String*, she was concerned about Hollywood's treatment of mysteries. She felt "it is worth it to make sure that the story does not receive the same type of mishandling that happened with RKO and *Having Wonderful Crime*."[16]

In addition to movies, Rice's work was featured on radio as well. *The Thursday Turkey Murders* aired in January 1944. Other of Rice's works, especially the Venning books, aired in 1944, purchased by the Molle Radio Theater. Several companies expressed interest in doing the Malone books on radio, although no one brought a deal together.

Rice presented a new Malone novel in 1945, *The Lucky Stiff*, one of Rice's personal favorites. The story concerns Anna Marie St. Clair, convicted of killing Big Joe Childers, her lover and a notorious Chicago crime boss. A last minute confession saves her from the electric chair, but she decides to allow the prison to make the announcement to the press that she had been executed. Returning to Chicago, she enlists Malone's help in finding out who framed her for the killing and seeking justice.

In this book, Malone comes as close as he ever does to falling in love. Malone lusted after numerous beautiful blondes in his adventures, but, at best, they were dalliances. This beautiful woman has no problem talking Malone into what she wants. "The tawny hair rippled on her shoulders when she moved her head. She was the most gorgeous girl Malone had ever seen and he'd seen a lot of gorgeous girls in his time. The whole picture of what had happened to her ran through his brain..."[17]

Pretending to be a ghost, Anna Marie wants to haunt all the people she suspects played a part in the plot to frame her. As she starts her plan, all the people who knew Anna Marie hadn't died start turning up dead. Malone suspects the girl that he finds himself falling in love with killed them, and vows to uncover the truth. "He knew what Anna Marie was doing. He knew why she was doing it. Frankly, he didn't blame her. But maybe he could talk her out of it. Because if she went ahead with what was undoubtedly in her mind, she was going to blow the lid off a political pot that was all ready to steam a little.

"It would destroy a number of his best connections if such a thing took place, but that wasn't his reason. He could always make new connections. It would ruin a number of his friends. Or were they his friends? Malone paused, razor in hand, and the lathered face that looked back at him from the mirror answered, 'No.'

"It might bring about a reform administration in the next election, and he'd have to find a new place to play poker. That had happened before, and he'd always managed.

"There would be danger to Anna Marie herself."[18]

Jake comes into the plot as the victim of an extortion plot against the Casino, and finds the protection racket tied to Anna Marie and Big Joe Childers' death.

The book doesn't hold together well. A man capable of being in love and caring for another person can't act as the amusing man-child that the reader has come to love. Malone has a depth of spirit, more in tune with Rice's shorter works than her novels. While the wisecracks and malapropisms appear, they stand out as inappropriate for a man involved in an adult relationship. A man in love doesn't joke about his intended. Originally, Rice left Jake and Helene out of *The Lucky Stiff*, but the cancellation of the *Countess* novel gave the public no Jake and Helene appearance for more than a year. So Rice went back and added the couple to her latest escapade. The two plots don't bisect as much as in the other books. Unfortunately, they detract from the story in this case and hurt the overall book.

In keeping with Rice's major theme, Anna Marie is another orphan who resents the world. Perhaps one of the reasons Rice favored this book stemmed from the fact that Anna Marie ends the novel by having haunted Chicago and starting a new career as a Hollywood starlet. Certainly Rice pulled off the plot device that hadn't stood up well in *Having Wonderful Crime*.

Without questions, Rice ghostwrote a mystery for someone whose path had crossed hers in Hollywood. Actor George Sanders wanted to try his hand at writing, and hired Rice to help him pen a mystery. The book has an interesting premise. George Sanders, long known to audiences as the Saint and the Falcon, tires of portraying detectives and wants a new, meatier role in the movies. In real life, Rice had co-authored Sanders' last Falcon picture, *The Falcon's Brother*. In the mid-1940s, Sanders was known primarily for his hero roles, which made him an ideal candidate for a fictional detective. Over the years, and through his many marriages (including those to both Magda and Zsa Zsa Gabor), he would play less attractive characters in such films as *The Picture of Dorian Gray*, and *All About Eve*. Although he played a cad in *Rebecca* just before meeting Rice, as he aged in the 1950s he became known for the villainous roles that seemed to suit him. In typical droll Sanders humor, he dedicated the book, "To Craig Rice, without whom this book could not have been written."

In dealing with her busy schedule, Rice hired her own ghost writer to complete the George Sanders book, *Crime on My Hands*. "I have a contract with George Sanders of which he is to pay me 50% of all royalties, reprint rights, etc. on *Crime on My Hands*. As you know, I have to split with my own ghost writer in this case."[18] From what can be determined, Cleve Cartmill, one of Rice's writing friends, completed the novel for Rice. Although he was basically known as a science-fiction/fantasy writer in the 1940s, Cartmill and Rice collaborated on a few projects, including an unsold novella called "Valse Triste For Calliope," a rather far-fetched mystery. They worked together on the plot of the story, with Cartmill doing the actual writing and Rice editing the first draft.

Fictionally, Sanders takes the role of Hilary Weston in a film called *Seven Dreams*. Almost immediately, a young man dies on the set, killed with a .38 caliber shot during the shooting of a scene, and Sanders finds himself the logical suspect due to the caliber of his guns. The cast had been given .45s and only the lead actor had received a .38. Sanders narrows down the list of suspects. Someone behind the camera had to pull the trigger, not one of the actors on the set. Sanders plays detective games with the canister of film that captured the murder. A truly Rician touch is the writer, so intimidated by the movie people that the crew mistakes him for an extra and bosses the poor man around. In the meantime, everyone searches for the missing writer, who should have shown up on the set days ago.

The book didn't live up to its promise. Rice bogged down the novel with too many pages spent admiring the fact that George Sanders was George Sanders, and not some mere mortal. "As *The Saint* and/or *The Falcon* I had been attracted by crimes not cast in the common mold. And as those super-sleuths, I always brought the culprit to bay. Justice prevailed,"[19] He even takes time to ruminate on how he might be a potential victim because he portrayed a detective on the screen. Anthony Boucher called the book a hack job and chided Rice and Cartmill for their effort. However, in her own mystery review column, Rice named *Crime on My Hands* as one of the ten best mystery novels of 1944, albeit number ten on the list. "Naturally, the book is full of fascinating Hollywood material and delightful Hollywood characters. The story is an exciting and mystifying one, with a high degree of humor."[20]

Craig Rice neglected to mention her part in the effort to the audience. She often crossed over from impartial reviewer to interested party by promoting her own books or reviewing the work of friends. In one review, she disparaged the most recent *Saint* novel by Leslie Charteris, who had ceased publication of her magazine.

Jethro Hammer, the last Michael Venning book, appeared in 1944, originally called *Long Time Dead* for the snippet of a song that ends the book. As expected from the Venning series, the book is a crime novel, but not the usual play-fair detective story. The book opens with the murderer carrying out his crime and later being arrested for it. The murderer hires Melville Fairr to discover why the police have settled on him, still unnamed to the reader, as the murderer.

Within this frame, which bookends the novel, Rice writes the life of another orphan. The telling of the story is tiered on three separate levels: the denouement that frames the book, the story of Fairr solving the crime, and the story of Jethro Hammer's life. Despite the multi-leveled approach, the writing flows easily between the stories and the reader has little difficulty in determining which of the levels is being told.

A sad story, the Donahue family adopts a foundling left in St. Joseph's church in Leesville, Ohio. The family names him for the church janitor and a tool in Will Donahue's shop. Jethro is not given the family name, and is thus established as being a part of and apart from an adopted family. The Donahue children make it known that he is never quite a member of their clan, although in most respects they treat him like kin.

When Will Donahue dies a wealthy man, Jethro has no claim on the estate. One of the brothers offers him a job as a chauffeur. He leaves for parts unknown, only to return twenty years later to reclaim the Donahue fortune (or Donohoughs, as they prefer to be called now). Will Donahue's diary shows that Hammer, not Will, Sr., had developed the invention which had made them all rich.

Ironically, at the time he died, Hammer had spent all of the Donahue millions attempting to find his real parents so that he might "fit" into the Donahue's world as an equal and ask for the hand of Sally Donahue, his boyhood love. On the day of his death, Jethro thinks he has found his true identity and calls the siblings he hasn't seen in years. Yet the Donahue children, who had all been left without a penny after lawsuits over the family fortune, learn they are much happier without the inherited wealth. The children have started working and being responsible members of society. They have made their own way at this point, no longer relying on their father's money.

The Donahue family takes to the little gray man, Mr. Fairr, and offers to pay him to find Hammer's killer. So Fairr has three offers for fees: the victim (who suspected he would be murdered) the true killer, and the suspects. Fairr only accepts the commission from Hammer, but still solves the various mysteries.

The book differs from the typical Malone books in the dearth of humor and the lack of mass quantities of alcohol. The laughs in Hammer come from the alibis for the Donahue family, most of who argue with and question the police interrogators. Each viewpoint is slightly varied, and the police have no easy question-and-answer sessions.

The book does have some Rician touches, though. Rice liked to point to her other books within each novel. The Venning pseudonym has its genesis in *The Right Murder*, where he appeared as a character. Will Donahue, Jr., a detective fiction buff, and Fairr discuss several mystery authors including "a dissertation on the latest book by Craig Rice."[21] Again Rice throws readers to another book penned by her hand, this time *Crime on My Hands*, with the alibi of Mr. Dawes. Dawes spoke with a director named Riegleman, one of the characters from the Sanders book.

As Rice's talent grew, she could better depict characters whose motivation stemmed from their lack of parents. Hammer, the most bereft orphan in the Rice canon, spends millions trying to find his name. "All he knew of himself was that he was alive and walked upon the earth."[22] The Hammer name lives on at the end of the book, as his daughter falls in love with and decides to marry one of Will, Jr.'s grandsons. Children with the Hammer bloodline, who know their parentage, will carry on the family name.

Alfred Fisher, an independent producer, wanted to buy the rights to *Jethro Hammer* for United Artists, but the deal fell through at the last minute. Some of the backers thought that casting would be near to impossible for the treatment, mostly likely because of the large cast and the budget necessary to hire them. There were five Donahue children listed in the book, as well as their families.

Hammer marked the end of the Venning books, which Rice found more satisfying, but less profitable than the Malone novels. By 1945, monetary concerns became paramount to the writer and Malone won out.

CHAPTER SEVEN

"His name is Larry Lipton and he smokes a great many smelly cigars"

The *Time* magazine article on January 28, 1946, put Rice alone in the world of mystery. No mystery writer before or after her has ever been the subject of a *Time* cover story. In the place usually reserved for the visage of Harry Truman or Winston Churchill, world leaders, Rice's face appeared. In merely seven years, Rice had conquered a male-dominated field. Sales of her books increased significantly with the national exposure.

Despite the misrepresentations and outright lies she fed them, Rice charmed the interviewers, and they wrote glowingly of the initial interviews. "Today, she is a very pretty brunette (she dyes her hair to keep it from turning grey) with a nice figure that goes well with her joie de vivre. Craig Rice thinks life is more fun than anything. She is full of the pixie to the point of daring."[1] Seductive and charming, Rice got away with outrageous lies. Her charisma and wit made the recipient feel he was the only person who mattered.

The interview incensed her husband, Larry Lipton, who considered himself to be the real writer in the family. He'd spent years trying to convince himself and everyone else of his importance, only to be bested by his wife. Although he lived off the royalties from Rice's books, Rice's husband thought of genre fiction as beneath contempt. He could not believe that *Time* would promote an author of her caliber, rather than someone of Lipton's talent.

However, the editors were impressed with Rice and her upcoming magazine, *Craig Rice Crime Digest*, to be published by Anson Bond Publishing. The magazine was planned as a monthly, featuring summary-styled reprints of mystery novels in the digest-sized magazine. Bond had been half of Bond-Charteris Enterprises, with Leslie Charteris of *The Saint* fame. Bond sold his interest to Rudy Vallee and started his own magazine. *Time* talked with Bond, a frustrated mystery writer himself, at length about his plans for the digest. Bond had assumed the aborted Bond-Charteris venture after their split.

Now that Charteris and Bond had dissolved their publishing concern, Anson Bond decided to come out with his own series of Rice magazines featuring stripped down novels. Bond had sold his share of Bond-Charteris to Rudy Vallee for $100,000 and their company was renamed Saint Enterprises (for Charteris' famous detective). Bond created his own firm, which he named Anson Bond Publications.

The sloppy result, *Craig Rice Crime Digest*, lasted only two issues. The magazine lacked artwork and pared the novels to a Spartan length of eighteen thousand words, when a typical mystery novel runs between sixty and eighty thousand words. The books were typically years old, and previously read by the types of readers who would follow a particular author.

Rice decided to add a true crime column to the magazine. In the vein of the Hearst articles, she wished to propose solutions to true crime cases that she found through the newspapers and other sources. Since the magazine published for such a short time, she couldn't indulge her desire. Rice's popularity, at its height only a year before, had started to dwindle with the lack of new books, and lackluster projects such as the digest.

The cover portrait, done by *Time* artist, Boris Artzybasheff, showed Rice's face along with a typewriter's keyboard. A masked six-armed apparition emanates from the keyboard, what Rice later called a "sextopus". Each arm carries a different murder weapon: a bottle of poison; a gun; a knife; a syringe; and a rope held between two hands.

The article, entitled "Mulled Murder With Spice," was re-written to exclude all of the stories that Mary Randolph had refuted. Hostility at being duped showed in the piece. The tone of the profile oozed with condescension, even allowing for the attitude towards women in the middle years of the century. "To her the era of peace just ending had meant a dozen years of bohemian life: three bungled attempts at marriage; innumerable failures to write poetry, novels and music; barely successful efforts to earn a living around newspapers; and some definite progress in helping local bohemians support the distilling industry."[2] The fact that those dozen years when Rice had tried to earn a living are typically called the Great Depression didn't appear in the article, and to have made any money in journalism was an accomplishment in the 1930s. Her poetry failures had been published in several anthologies and won small press awards.

The author's tone reflected the uncomfortable feel of the article. Between the lines was a feeling that nice women shouldn't be doing this. "Had Craig Rice conceived a child instead of an idea"[3] and "She was the only woman I ever met who could crochet, play chess, read a book ... and hold a highball."[4] were typical quotes in the article about Rice. Trying to make this author into something other than Craig Rice wouldn't be an easy job. She didn't fit the Rosie the Riveter mold coming out of World War II, of a woman who happily returned to the kitchen when her man came home from the war. Nor did she fit the housewife mold, with her drinking and many husbands. Her personality made her unique - made her famous - and toning her down for national exposure made for difficult editing.

The article does compliment Rice's work, and would be interesting if only for its discussion of the war years mystery field. There is talk of the top practitioners of the genre, and the elite. "The few who do so [sell over 20,000 hardback copies] are authors who draw on the nondetective story audience; such exceptions as Mary Roberts Rinehart, Dorothy Sayers, and of course Gypsy Rose Lee . . ."[5] Several paragraphs explain the reprints market. Rice had recently signed contracts with Pocket Books, pointing out that very high sales of paperbacks only led to royalties of a few thousand dollars. Only a few of Rice's titles were published in paperback at that point.

The article in *Time* didn't make everyone in the mystery world happy. Fred Dannay, half of Ellery Queen, wrote a letter of protest to the magazine, referencing two statements he disagreed with. The article had stated that women excel in the mystery-writing field. Considering his own gender and status in the genre, Dannay protested the concentration in the piece on women mystery writers such as Gypsy Lee and Mary Roberts Rinehart. He also objected to references about the lack of mystery short fiction markets, and Rice's lack of output in the short story field. Rice had written "His Heart Could Break" for *Ellery Queen's Mystery Magazine* in March of 1943. Dannay's fledgling magazine needed all the publicity and respect it could get, and he corrected *Time*.

Other writers found fault with the *Time* article. Erle Stanley Gardner, for one, had been interviewed as early as 1934 about his success and prolific output in the mystery genre. However, the magazine had chosen not to run the piece after it was written. Other writers had similar experiences, only to see Rice's face on the magazine in 1946.

Unfortunately, success did not make her personal life run smoothly. Shortly after the article, Nan Rice was hospitalized. About the same time, Rice and Lipton decided to divorce. The situation with Lipton had deteriorated into frequent fist fights and screaming matches, fueled by alcohol. Rice moved out in early 1946 and decided to get a divorce. Among the reasons given for the break-up were Lipton's abusive behavior to the children and his abuse of her income.

In 1945, Rice had earned over $46,000 by writing, and the couple had spent roughly twelve thousand of that redoing the house and yard. The rest had disappeared into their parties and lifestyle, Lipton's separate office space, and more. Of their combined income, Lipton had made next to nothing, and yet continued the expensive pretense of writing. In addition, Rice entrusted Lipton with the checking account, and that frequently turned up empty when there should have been sufficient funds to pay the bills.

Lipton suffered a mental collapse shortly after the split. The couple reconciled briefly while he received help for a nervous breakdown. Brief reconciliations marked a pattern for Rice. She had difficulty with separation, rooted in her early unstable family life. The spiral of each separation caused her to go into a deeper depression, worsened by drinking. Rice decided to give Lipton six months to see if his mental recovery would improve their relationship. For a few months, Lipton seemed to improve, but the situation deteriorated into bitter fighting again.

Not only had Lipton spent her money and physically abused Rice, he'd also given her some unwanted notoriety. His longstanding affiliation with the local Communist party had come to the attention of the F.B.I. when Rice became popular. The couple had hosted a number of parties in their home for the Thomas Jefferson Bookstore in Santa Monica, which had ties to local Communist groups. Rice's interest in true crime, and requests for crime scene information only fueled the Feds' suspicions of evil deeds. The Feds monitored the group carefully in the time after the World War II. Spies infiltrated the group (to report back to the Feds), and went as far as to search Rice's home during the parties for clues to the strength of her affiliation. Even after the divorce, the F.B.I maintained a file on her. Years later, during the McCarthy era, facts about Lipton's involvement with the Communist Party would come out from undercover spies who attended the parties. Despite being characterized as not "know[ing] what the word moral meant" and his "inability to give short concise answers" by the spies, Lipton denied any knowledge of fundraising, or distributing "Red" literature.

The divorce became a particularly ugly affair, with charges and counter-charges. Rice had been spared a nasty court fight in her first two involvements. Her acrimonious relationship with Lipton would prove different. Lipton requested alimony from his wife, and demanded half of her earnings from the time they were married.

Ironically, Lipton sued for divorce on the grounds on mental cruelty. He cited Rice's manic behavior, saying, "It was murder. I could never get a decent night's sleep."[6] Rice stayed up typing into the night on a regular basis. She told friends that she could write for three or four days with little sleep to finish a book. Lipton told the courts during the divorce that he'd been relegated to an inferior position in the household, and had been humiliated by Rice's interruptions and comments about him.

The break-up of the marriage led Rice further into her depression and halted her writing altogether. In 1946 and 1947 combined, Rice did not write a single novel. The woman who had been churning out four novels a year dried up as the divorce and the depression wore on. Her old friend, Stuart Palmer, had re-enlisted in the army at this point, and wrote to congratulate her on the divorce. As much as he enjoyed Rice, Stuart despised Lipton. Stuart had served in the army during the war and was currently helping the army with motion pictures. At his new desk job, he started to write again and soon finished *Miss Withers Regrets*. He frequently complained to Rice that he had tired of his detective and wished to be rid of the old maid.

The divorce didn't help Rice's financial status. Simon & Schuster editor Lee Wright became increasingly infuriated with Rice's demands for more money and loans against her advances. Rice had promised *The Monday Mongoose Murders* (the similar title to Jake's book in *Wonderful Crime*), *Shirtsleeves* (an unidentified work), and *The Fourth Postman*. The people at Dial Press continued to inquire into the status of *Time to Kill*, supposedly the second in the Daphne Sanders series. Rice had already spent the advance without writing a word. Despite the open ending of *To Catch a Thief*, Rice never began a sequel featuring John Moon and Donovan.

Rice's sole source of royalties from her books became the rapidly growing foreign markets. In a single year, Rice had sold the French, Dutch, Danish, German, Swedish, and Norwegian rights to several of her novels. Rice delighted in the copies of her books in languages she couldn't read. Since the foreign markets (even though new and rather unreliable in payment) seemed promising, Rice frequently planned for money that didn't come through when she wanted it, leaving her tangled in debt.

Rice's attention turned away from her personal and financial problems with the start of a new radio program, *Murder and Mr. Malone*. Rice told her friends to listen to the show on the Los Angeles radio station, KECA. The series began on January 11th, 1947 and starred Frank Lovejoy as John J. Malone. Rice wrote the pilot for the series, adapted for the half-hour format. Airing at 9:30 Saturday night as the Guild Wine show, the on-air Malone differed from the novel character. He was "five-tenths charm, two-tenths nice voice, two-tenths brains and nerve, and two-tenths plain old sex appeal."[7] Despite the recipe, Malone was a vanilla character, devoid of the stumbling charm of the books. In keeping tabs on Rice, the F.B.I. read a copy of her script before allowing ABC to air the show.

To take her mind off of the separation and divorce, Rice took a turn as a true crime journalist, working for Hearst and the *Los Angeles Herald-Express*. Long before she sold novels or became a *Time* cover story, Rice had covered trials as a court reporter in her youth. As a mystery author, she generated news when she appeared at a crime scene. One of the more famous cases Rice dabbled in involved William Heirens, accused of killing six-year old Suzanne Degnan of Chicago. The little girl had been kidnapped in January 1946, and police later found her dismembered body. Clues from the ransom note puzzled Chicago's finest for weeks until they settled on Heirens, a student at the University of Chicago.

The story made headlines in the Windy City for weeks. Confusion reigned when another man admitted to the crimes, but his fingerprints didn't match the ransom note. When Heirens was taken to the hospital following an arrest for a break-in, he "confessed" to the crime under the influence of sodium pentothal and the newspapers went wild with the story of a truth serum confession. The Chicago papers decided that Heirens was guilty, and ran stories about his possible implication in other murders.

Although Chicago had judged him guilty in the press, Rice came into town convinced the boy was innocent and even volunteered to undergo an experimental injection of the truth serum to determine if a confession could be coerced out of someone under its influence. "... I would like to see those same worthwhile youths convinced that the citizens of Chicago believe in justice, and not in lynch law. I would rather see them mistakenly believe Bill Heirens is a martyr than to have them make the shocking discovery that an innocent Bill Heirens was actually made a martyr because it was necessary to find someone guilty of two brutal crimes."[8] She upset a number of Chicago bureaucrats with demands for exclusive interviews. The local politicians cringed at the thought of a stranger getting all the press in the high publicity case.

Rice put herself in an awkward position with her notoriety and demands, and resorted to unethical means to make her deadlines. Erle Stanley Gardner recalls, "The thing that made me furious, however, was the fact that when a story blew up in her [Rice] back in Chicago and she had to think of something else quick, she decided to interview her various 'competitors' about the case. I received through the mail a copy of the paper containing my picture and the things I had said to her about the case, the interview making me seem to be very much of a stuffed shirt. She explained to me that she didn't have any opportunity to get in touch with me, so she had an imaginary interview and tried to think of things I would have said if I had been talking at the other end of the line.

"I blew up and gave it to her with both barrels. . . To my mind the irritating part of all this publicity stuff is not the legitimate publicity but the attempt to push herself into the limelight and milk the situation dry."[9] The situation was made worse by the fact that Gardner had been passed up on *Time* interview.

Almost six months to the day from the cover story, *Time* ran another article about Craig Rice. *Time* wrote, "Wuxtry! Read All About It!" about the mystery writer, this time pulling no punches. The slant of the article made Rice look like a fool; coming into town, making a lot of noise and leaving town with her tail between her legs. They called her "plump, popeyed Craig Rice looking for clues —. . ."[10] Comparing her to newspaper woman Hildy Johnson (of the film *His Girl Friday* fame), the article spoke about the professional behavior of the local papers vs. the out-of-town crowd's antics. The article as well as the public spectacle over the trial ended when "A few days later she made good on her [Rice's] promise to steal out of town."[11] Rice's teenaged children wrote a letter to the editor complaining about the treatment of their mother in the magazine, and the editor apologized in print for the harsh descriptions of the author.

Undaunted, Rice covered another high profile case in the Newport Bay area of California in which a boat (with the owner onboard) exploded, allegedly with assistance from the owner's daughter and her boyfriend. Rice covered the case along with a number of crime writers, including Adela Rogers St. Johns (who had written about the Lindbergh kidnapping case). This assignment would be

Rice's last Hearst assignment.

Her features ran for several months in the newspapers, and then the news syndicate summarily fired Rice. Rice had put more time and effort into the investigating than the writing. The effects of alcohol caused Rice to pump out unrevised articles and stories, poorly written work that usually found its way to the inside pages of the newspaper. Despite her status in the world of mystery writing, she had only been paid on the Guild scale for her work. Her pay had been that of a cub reporter. Even so, the Hearst syndicate felt they weren't getting their money's worth from Rice.

Having a taste of true crime, Rice edited *Los Angeles Murders* in 1947. Duell, Sloan, and Pierce had published a series of regional true crime books and Rice had submitted a piece for Marie Rodell's *Chicago Murders*. Typically, local authors wrote a short piece on a true crime case that fascinated them in the titular city.

Rice's introduction highlighted L.A.'s true crime past with a running travelogue. Her comic premise stated that something set Los Angeles apart from the rest of the nation, an intangible element that made it special and different. ". . . Los Angeles was founded by an explorer who was trying to find someplace else. . . On the site of what is now a well known Los Angeles park, he [the explorer] ran into a village of curious little people who were like no other aborigines on the North American continent. (Even in those days, Los Angeles had to be different!)"[12] Rice goes on to recount the first murder in L.A,. and several other homicide cases that had intrigued the authors but didn't make the book.

For the L.A. book, Erle Stanley Gardner wrote about the William Desmond Taylor case, in which the famous Hollywood director of the 1920s died mysteriously at this home. Showing the seamy side of the flappers and the movie world, Gardner (who also worked as part of the famous Court of Last Appeals) pointed out the flaws in the police investigation. Mystery writers Mary Collins, George Yates, and Guy Endore wrote other stories.

From her mystery review column and projects like *Los Angeles Murders*, Rice introduced herself to a number of local writers, especially mystery authors in California. As a result of her connections, Rice became instrumental in starting the Southern California chapter of

Mystery Writers of America. She flew to New York several times to attend monthly meetings, but found the trip tiring. Always one to enjoy a party, she helped to gather her writing friends to discuss the business of writing mysteries under the auspices of MWA. (Their motto was "Crime does not pay - enough!") Rice had been installed on the Board of Directors of MWA in 1946, along with her friends Anthony Boucher and Dorothy B. Hughes. Rice spoke at one of the New York meetings about the difficulty of turning a mystery novel into a film, a subject she knew painfully well.

Her popularity continued to rise as *Home Sweet Homicide* hit the theaters in 1946. The movie, the closest adaptation of her work, starred Western hero Randolph Scott as the homicide detective assigned to the murder case and Lynn Bari as Marian. The movie, filmed by 20th Century Fox, had Rice as a script consultant on the film. Rice had expressed concern for the work after the hatchet job on *Having Wonderful Crime*.

The children visited Rice on the set, and attended the opening of the movie at Grauman's Chinese Theater. Rice, proud of the work, took the whole family to the premiere of the film in a taxi. Rice had never learned to drive and the family always traveled to Los Angeles in a cab. With the heavy drinking that the Liptons did, not having a license seemed reasonable.

The movie contained the same Carstairs children and the same murderer. However, Hollywood modified the plot drastically by altering the motive for the killing and removing most of the book's subplots. Even little details such as the number of O'Hara children were changed for no reason.

After the *Time* interview with photographs of Rice and her family, the movie producers took great pains to cast actors who resembled their real life counterparts. Lynn Bari could double for the mystery writer with her shoulder length brown hair, bangs curled up, and long face. Rice posed for a photograph about this time, and her glamorous looks and mink coat made her look like a movie star. The children resemble their characters as well, with a curly haired Dean Stockwell playing the fictional Archie.

Rice had enjoyed the past few years with her children, but even this short period was interspersed with long absences. At fifteen, David attended military school in Colorado. In Rice-like fashion, she forgot to pay the tuition and David would be reprimanded for her transgression. Nancy lived at an all-girls Catholic convent in Los Angeles.

While in high school, Nancy had met and fallen in love with Joseph Atwill. Atwill was a young man from the Santa Monica neighborhood, and the couple married in June 1946 shortly after Nancy's eighteenth birthday. Atwill had finished school and worked for his family's chemical company. He had been raised a Catholic, and Rice became increasingly interested in the religion. After their marriage, Joe and Nancy Atwill moved in with Rice. Nancy took care of the house and Rice, while the author tried to jumpstart her career.

The household grew again when Nancy Atwill gave birth to a daughter, Anne Elizabeth, on April 26, 1947. Rice sent out telegrams to her friends in mystery (Ned Guymon, A.P. White, and Fred Dannay, among others) and posed for pictures at the typewriter with the baby on her lap.

The divorce proceedings with Lipton dragged on for over a year. Lipton wanted half of Rice's earnings, claiming that he had given Rice the ideas for her mysteries and had written most of the true crime pieces. No mention was made of Rice's short stories, which match the novels in tone and style. Lipton's lawyer asked for half of all royalties as community income, even for the books written before Lipton and Rice met or married. Given Lipton's hostility to Rice and her work, his claims don't hold up. Lipton considered himself an artist, and literary fiction has long looked down its nose at genre fiction. Most likely, Lipton feared losing the source of funds that had supplied him with the luxuries of life for many years. The stress of the divorce led Rice to have a collapse brought on by alcohol, and left her in the hospital for several days in the weeks before the divorce.

Rice countered Lipton's charges with claims of child abuse. During Rice's drinking, Lipton had run the house and the children. At one point during the marriage, a social services worker visited the house to investigate charges of abuse, but Rice refused to pursue the issue. Only when the divorce began did Rice choose to use abuse as a counter-charge. It would be two more decades before Lipton would put his ideas on paper about sex and the so-called sexual revolution of the 1960s. He believed in a laissez-faire attitude towards sex.

Rice's only output during this tumultuous time was a Michael Venning short story called "How Now, Ophelia" that appeared in *Ellery Queen's Mystery Magazine*. It was the only short work published under the Venning pseudonym. Rice would write another Fairr story, but didn't do much with the series in the shorter form because she felt that Fred Dannay didn't care for the Fairr stories. Dannay preferred her short Malone pieces, which ranked among her best work.

The story has a Shakespearean theme, something the Malone series could never have gotten away with, but it fit well with the more stylized Venning series. "Ophelia" concerns Lucia Cattermole, an orphan who lives with her stepfather, Jesse, a retired actor, and her husband, Bart Cannon, a big drunken brute who physically abuses his wife. Lucia loves Tony Gay, the neighbor, who is also a member of the family that once owned the land that Cannon now owns. The years of physical abuse have driven Lucia to the edge of sanity, hence the references to Hamlet and Ophelia, and she has made attempts to kill her husband. Jesse hires Melville Fairr to prevent the murder of Bart Cannon. While Fairr debates whether to take the case, Cannon is murdered. Fairr helps the local police solve the case. The reader needs little imagination to determine how Rice came up with the idea of killing an abusive spouse.

After the divorce became final in April 1947, Rice met a young screenwriter whose career she helped through her connections in publishing. Henry "Hank" DeMott was eleven years younger than Rice, twenty-nine to her forty, but she quickly took up company with him. Rice, dependent on men in part because of her bipolar disorder, needed constant male companionship. Just as she had sent Lipton's work to her agent and friendly reviewers, Rice introduced DeMott to her agent and her editor, trying to encourage others to help DeMott 's career. She even offered to write a novelization of one of his screenplays that she believed could be published.

DeMott was not the only novice writer Rice helped. Rice taught a class for young writers towards the end of 1947. She interviewed and selected students for a class she entitled, "Techniques of the Mystery Story and Radio Script Writing". The class met at the San Diego School of Arts and Crafts in La Jolla. Orin and Marian Louden, Bertie Ferguson's sister, had founded the school. The Loudens were the relatives that Ferguson had visited shortly before his heart attack, and Rice kept in touch with them after she moved to Los Angeles. One of Rice's students sent an article to the Ann Watkins Agency along with a note from Rice. Rice's enthusiasm for the weekly class bubbled over to the students who wrote for her. Since Rice didn't drive, the trip became long and tedious. The effort folded after a few months. Rice seemed to enjoy teaching; however, she didn't have the time to help the students properly.

The note to her agent seemed only to emphasize that Rice had not written anything. Jean Macy had taken over Rice's account, and spent a good deal of her time playing bank teller to Rice and her never-ending money problems.

Despite the lack of new work, Rice continued to promote herself and her work. She was her own best publicity machine. When a fan from Colombia, South America, sent her a twelve-foot boa constrictor. Rice quickly named the snake Malone and posed with it for pictures before giving the reptile to a local animal shop. Shortly after that, the boa gave birth to 72 baby boas, setting a scientific record. Again Rice posed with the children of Malone as they slithered across her desk, typewriter, and books. After the photo shoot, the animal keepers had to dismantle the typewriter to return all of the young snakes back to the pet store.

CHAPTER **E I G H T**

"Nobody, including Craig Rice, seems to remember much about her husbands."

In April 1948, Rice decided to wed again, this time to Hank DeMott, who accompanied Rice everywhere now. The couple vacationed often in Mexico prior to the wedding, enjoying what Rice called a "pre-honeymoon." Rice married a younger man on her fourth trip to the altar, breaking her pattern of older men, although she maintained her streak of only marrying writers.

Rice's first wedding as a famous author became a splashy event. The wedding took place in the library of Ned Guymon's home in San Diego on May 1, 1948, amidst the thousands of mystery first editions. The Guymons footed the bill for the extravaganza, and Rice went all-out, inviting famous guests and making sure that the press attended in droves. Rice had married Lipton just after *8 Faces at 3* hit the book-stands, so the DeMott wedding was her first media event marriage.

Ned Guymon recalled, "At the time, I was walking with the help of a cane because of a knee injury, but I managed to hobble along and deliver Rice to Hank. Then I stepped around, became best man and was able to hand Hank the ring without fumbling. . . . At the conclusion of the ceremony, Rice autographed copies of *Stiff* and we adjourned to the dining room."[1]

The wedding had a mystery motif. Guymon gave away the bride, and she carried a copy of *The Lucky Stiff*, her most recent work and a personal favorite, with her down the aisle instead of a Bible. The wedding cake sported a string of miniature skulls around the top tier.

The couple never went on a honeymoon.

Now happily ensconced in a relationship again, Rice returned to her work in a particularly manic way. Rice was busy writing. She worked on the radio show, which had recently lost the sponsor and undergone a name change to *The Amazing Mr. Malone.* Frank Lovejoy continued portraying the on-air John J. Malone.

Rice's newfound happiness quickly disintegrated. Shortly after the marriage, Rice discovered that Lipton had not paid their income taxes in 1946 or 1947, two of Rice's biggest moneymaking years. The IRS intervened and put Rice on a strictly imposed budget of forty-five dollars a week. She worked out the details with a financial advisor and her agents.

While it was possible to maintain a decent lifestyle on a little over $2000 a year in 1948, the financial restraints proved disastrous to Rice. She had known no ends to her success and always seemed to be at loose ends for cash. Rice had made almost $50,000 in 1946 and over $25,000 in the year before. The government took all the Rice assets. She tried desperately to save the house she loved, but in the end she sold it to pay off debts. Rice lost money on the house sale, only getting $22,500 for the house and the lot next to it. Most of the cash went to pay off Lipton's second trust deed, a part of the property settlement to Lipton, the original mortgage, and a portion owed for government taxes. The DeMotts also sold their car and purchased a used MG for Hank DeMott. Guymon couldn't bail Rice out of her latest problems, having suffered financial difficulties of his own. His letters to Rice became more formal, lecturing to her on the value of a budget. Guymon wasn't sympathetic to people who didn't pay their income taxes.

"Frankly, I called you because again I am in one hell of a jam — and I wanted to make sure this would reach you.

"Naturally, it's money. (It always is, with me!) As usual, there is money coming in — but not available in time. . .

    "Altogether, Ned, I need to borrow just about $500. In security I can offer a lien on any monies coming in not already tagged by the Income Tax Bureau. There certainly will be that much coming in within 60 days. Can you do it? Plus regular interest, of course, and with a properly signed note, and whatever else you need 'wrote down on a piece'a paper'"[2]

    Nan Rice moved out of the house and into a little apartment near Nancy and her growing family. Rice paid the rent in advance out of the money from the house sale. Craig and Nan Rice had not been getting along well. The distance improved their relationship. Nan Rice didn't approve of Craig Rice's lifestyle or her excessive drinking, which only seemed to increase as the years went on.

    Rice, DeMott, and son David moved into a small cabin at Big Bear Lake. DeMott sacrificed his writing career to get a job selling vacuum cleaners door to door. Rice tried to put the best possible face on her plight by telling friends that she wanted to live a simpler life with DeMott.

    "First, I wish you could see my little menage. After years of having a fourteen room house, a housekeeper, a secretary, three telephones and stuff, and being miserable - we now have the most heavenly little log house up in the .... Mountains! There, I knew I could do it! I said little - well, I guess it seems little by comparison with the white elephant down in Santa Monica. There's a big living room with a fireplace made of native rock, native pine walls, etc. Hank got inspired and built me a bookcase, record cabinet, and radio-phonograph cabinet combination that covers one wall, up to about 3 feet from the floor. The upper part of was just plain wallboard so he got a flock of regional air charts, in gorgeous colors, and papered the wall with them. The result is beautiful! Also downstairs there is a kitchen which is my favorite room in the house. (You'd be surprised what a good cook I am.) Also a small and comfortable bedroom (Maybe I should say the kitchen is my second favorite room in the house!) and a very comfortable and utilitarian study where I am now working. Also a bathroom downstairs. Upstairs there are two bedrooms and a bath, which we are going to remodel a little. All this, and furnished too, for $75 a month."[3]

Big Bear Lake provided some insulation from the world for the couple. Hours from Santa Monica, the town is situated northeast of Los Angeles, in the mountains. The log cabins and quaint shops sit on the rim of a large lake that gives the town its name. Nothing could be further from the frenetic pace of Los Angeles and Hollywood, which Rice had enjoyed.

To add insult to audit, Ozzie and Harriet Nelson sued Rice in June 1948. Rice had taken $2500 as an advance to write a script for their radio show. In typical fashion, she had accepted the money without producing any work. The couple waited nearly two years to sue, but with the IRS taking its share, the radio stars decided to wait no longer.

Rice's new business manager worked out a payment plan with Simon & Schuster and paid off the IRS. Lee Wright was ecstatic to have Rice off her back, requesting constant accountings and advances to tide her over. Rice started writing again in hopes that the books would help her out financially. New books (that weren't half-owned by Larry Lipton) would improve her income. Rice still promised her publisher that she would finish *The Monday Mongoose Murders*, and actually pitched an idea for a mystery set in Big Bear. Ironically, Rice wrote to Guymon about her next Malone book, *My Kingdom for a Hearse*. Almost ten years would pass before she would complete that novel.

Rice wrote another Melville Fairr story for Fred Dannay, one that would never see publication in the magazine. In notes about the work, Rice revealed that the victim died from too much sex. Dannay hesitated, writing the "Modus Operandi of the murder in the Venning story would certainly get us in trouble with the post office authorities."[4] Guymon countered that the story gave "a different meaning to Howard Haycraft's title 'Murder for Pleasure'."[5] The story was called "Eyes Up In Moonlight" and Rice used the story as collateral for another small loan from Guymon, who enjoyed the story immensely. The work became a private joke between the pair. "And if I can't talk Fred [Dannay] into publishing it in spite of the fact that the victim was literally F——d (sic) to death —- I shall send you the original, as a Christmas present — 'the most unpublished story by Craig Rice'."[6]

Rice wrote longer works as well. Her first book in almost three years was a Malone/Justus mystery, *The Fourth Postman*. Rice claimed to have been inspired for this book by Fred Dannay's postcards, and the plot impetus shows. The whole novel has a Queenian flair: the odd family relationships; people who are thought to be dead or missing actually living on the premises; a very closed environment of three adjacent homes; and a provision in a will requiring the permission of all three owners before one of them can sell their property.

"'He got married,' Kenneth said, 'and he had Uncle Rodney. I don't know much about Uncle Rodney's mother, but I've seen her picture. She was pretty. She died, and he got married again, and had Uncle Ernie. That wife died too. He got married again—'

'This begins to sound like the first chapter of Matthew,' Malone said, 'but go on'"[7]

Three postmen are killed in the alley just outside of the Farifaxx house to prevent letters arriving from a presumed dead ex-love of Rodney Fairfaxx. When the police deduce Rodney committed the crimes, von Flanagan, who now plans to be an actor, calls in Malone to defend the millionaire, in one of the few instances when Malone and von Flanagan are on the same side of the law. Helene shows up to support her friends, the Fairfaxxes, and Jake knows Rodney's nephew's ex-wife, who worked at the Casino. The trio teams up with a mutt that they call an "Australian beer hound" which everyone wants to adopt at first sight.

This typical Rice yarn has the three heroes going off in all directions at once. Jake has the chicken pox, turns up missing, and tries to solve the case on his own. Malone is kidnapped and nailed to the basement wall of one of the houses. "Malone groaned, and wished he were dead. Obviously someone had exploded a cannon cracker inside his skull, and he could still taste the fumes.

"He tried experimentally to move, and decided that he was dead. No, on second thought, only partially so. He could move his legs, with a little difficulty. But his feet didn't seem quite to touch any solid substance. There was something solid down there, but it was maddeningly out of reach.

"He opened his eyes. Utter darkness.

"He sniffed the air. There was an odor of musty wood, damp concrete, and old mice.

"After a few minutes, he decided that he was alive. Just where, and why, he wasn't sure. There was a splitting ache in his head, but he couldn't move it."[8]

This incident comes as close to real danger to life and limb as Malone ever finds in any of the novels. Even in *Postman*, the mutt soon saves him.

Overall this novel must be labeled one of Rice's lesser works, as the plot twists and the family tree of the Fairfaxxes is almost unintelligible. Although some Rician elements surface, in the relationship between Glida and Kenneth's misunderstanding and the mutt scenes, the plot resembles a traditional Golden Age puzzle more than a Rice "fast and furious" mystery. The blending doesn't go over well and the book disappoints.

Even Rice admitted that the novel didn't mesh well, "Now about the business of Jake being missing. Frankly, Lee, Jake has ben [sic] a fifth wheel all through this book. In that long sequence there's just wasn't a damn thing to do with him. When I wrote that sequence, to be honest, I didn't know how the hell I would wind it up. But it was a way of keeping Jake in the story by keeping him out of it, if you know what I mean. Then it occurred to me that building up to a perfect letdown might be the answer. Really I like it this way. But - I can easily rewrite it."[9]

As noted in a previous quote, Rice includes references to the Bible in *The Fourth Postman*. Although she included other religious quotes and quips in her books (such as the nine sons of Chris Halvorson named for the first nine books of the New Testament, Matthew to Second Corinthians), Rice used more frequent mentions of religious humor and references in her later novels. The interest in religion spilled over into her personal life as well. Rice wrote to her friends at Christmas in 1948, requesting that they not send gifts to her, but to write checks to the Fathers of St. Edmund, an orphanage in Alabama. Despite her divorces and her alcohol problem, the Catholic Church fascinated Rice.

Rice's second book in 1948, *Innocent Bystander*, had originally been called *Murder-Go-Round*, but Simon & Schuster discovered another book with that title and made a last minute name change. One of Rice's few non-series works, the novel was much grittier than most of her canon. *Innocent Bystander* involves the killing of a crime boss on a Ferris wheel at a small-time carnival in California. "Fun and fear go hand-in-hand in the amusement parks. Because it's fun to be frightened. Scare yourself into fits on the Sky Ride - perhaps this will be the one time when a car jumps the tracks and skids into the ocean. Or this will be the time the boat, coming down the chutes, will capsize when it hits the water. Or maybe this time the Diving-Bell won't come up again.

This time something had happened.

A man had been found dead on the Ferris wheel, and the police were there to ask questions."[10]

Rice reworked the plot of *The Lucky Stiff* here. The hero and the boss's girl must clear themselves of the gangster's murder. This time, Jerry McGurn is murdered, and Tony Webb and Ellen Haven are the suspects. However, the plot similarities end there, because the book lacks humor; the characters are serious.

The idea of the anti-hero wasn't new for Rice; *To Catch a Thief* offered a robber-hero as the protagonist. However, she took the concept to a new level in *Innocent Bystander*. Policeman Art Smith wants to subvert the law for the woman he thinks he loves. Without much thought, he tries to frame Tony Webb for the murders. In her previous books, the law was mainly ineffective, not corrupt. On the other hand, Webb decides to finger the murderer because the killer had done away with Amby, the speech-impaired carny caricaturist. Tony was unaffected by the killings of McGurn, the man who had stiffed him for $50,000, or the crooked cop. Amby, as an innocent, is the only victim worth mourning or avenging.

While the plot lacks originality for Rice, her style definitely changed. The staccato sentences shoot like a mobster's gun. The dialogue reflects more realistic conversation, with characters talking in short thoughts and interrupting each other. Rice wrote no other book in this manner, although many of her non-series short stories bear stylistic similarities, as do most of the true crime pieces she wrote during this time. Some of the short stories read like police reports.

"Her eyes. Art Smith laughed a little. He knew they were blue. He imagined them with long, dark, curling lashes. Wicked, inviting, hinting, fascinating eyes. It seemed for a moment almost as though they winked at him.

"No, definitely not a good girl.

"Art Smith sighed.

"He wondered how soon he would find her."[11]

While the change is interesting, *Innocent Bystander* remains an average hardboiled novel. By now, her readers expected a certain type of mystery and were disappointed by her attempts to do something different with her craft. She excelled at the comical farce detective story, but only stood as one among many hardboiled writers.

Despite Rice's output to help the family, in the end, the DeMotts' marriage proved no match for the financial strains. By March 1949, the couple separated and later reconciled. The pattern of fight and make-up continued throughout this relationship. Rice came down with pneumonia and had to stay in bed for several weeks. The additional pressure of Rice being ill didn't help their marriage.

To make matters worse, Nan Rice fell down a flight of stairs, tearing a ligament in her leg, and Rice gave up the house in Big Bear to stay with her. Still strapped for cash, Rice couldn't nurse Nan Rice and write at the same time. While she tended to her adoptive mother, DeMott left for Florida to try to straighten out some business matters. Rice lost more income when *The Amazing Mr. Malone* went off the air in late March 1949.

When DeMott and Rice left Big Bear separately, they both neglected to take David with them. David remained in Big Bear. The boy, only seventeen at the time, washed dishes for a living and slept above the tavern where he worked. Nancy and Joe Atwill went up to visit him in the small town. Within a few months, David decided to join the Navy. Rice helped David to enlist by creating a false birth certificate. Soon after entry, he took an aptitude test and discovered that he scored exceptionally high in electronics. He left for a year in the Electronics training program. From the program, he went on to three years in the Orient.

The DeMotts reconciled briefly in the summer, moving to Ventura. They stayed in a small apartment, tapping Ned Guymon for more financial help. Rice continued to sell short stories, a form that took more of her time as she tried to make money. Lipton hadn't bothered to include any of the form in his divorce settlement.

Rice's active mind could come up with a multitude of story ideas in a very short time. One of the stories that saw publication in *Ellery*

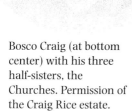

Bosco Craig (at bottom center) with his three half-sisters, the Churches. Permission of the Craig Rice estate.

Nancy (on the right) and Iris while living with Nan and Elton. Permission of the Craig Rice estate.

Craig (in black) just after her return to Nan and Elton Rice. Permission of the Craig Rice estate.

Craig. Permission of the Craig Rice estate.

Bohemian pose of Craig (actually pregnant with Nancy). Permission of the Craig Rice estate.

Elton Rice and Craig. Permission of the Craig Rice estate.

Jeffrey A. Marks

Film Poster for Home Sweet Homicide (in Spanish, Craig loved those foreign rights). Permission of the Craig Rice estate.

Time Magazine Cover, January 28, 1946. Permission of Time Magazine. Copyright Time Magazine 1946

Who Was That Lady?

Bosco as an adult. Permission of the Craig Rice estate.

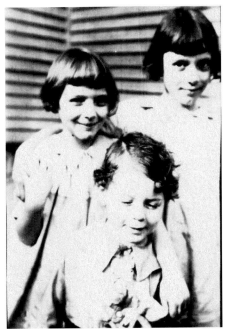

Nancy (on the right), Iris, and David. Permission of the Craig Rice estate.

Craig Rice Publicity Photo. Copyright Philipe Halsman. Permission of Harry and Miriam McNabb.

Craig and Hank DeMott at their wedding. Permission of Bowling Green State University, Popular Culture library, Guymon collection.

Craig and Ned Guymon. Permission of Bowling Green State University, Popular Culture library, Guymon collection.

Permission of USC, Lipton Collection.

Permission of USC, Lipton Collection.

Craig Rice Publicity Photo.

Craig's desk at her last apartment. UCLA, Special Collections Library, LA Times archive. Permission of the Craig Rice estate.

Bosco's painting of Mary Craig. Permission of Howard Metcalfe.

Queen's Mystery Magazine was "The Bad Luck Murders," which Rice sold as an original (even though an almost identical version of the story had appeared in *Baffling Detective Mysteries* in 1943 as "Dead Men's Shoes"). She had changed parts of the first few paragraphs to mask a cursory glance at the story, but left the rest of the work intact. Assuming cash would save her marriage, as it had prolonged her union with Lipton, Rice resorted to unethical business behavior with her friends.

In early 1949, Stuart Palmer moved to Chula Vista, California, close enough for Rice to visit her old friend. They quickly came up with the idea to team their sleuths, Malone and Hildegarde Withers, together in a series of short stories. Palmer had wearied of his creation and referred to her now as an old battle-ax. The thought of writing about another detective appealed to Palmer. No pair of authors had ever thought to combine their literary creations prior to this, and the series was incredibly successful. Yet, the idea has rarely been repeated. Ed Hoch did a series of stories for *Ellery Queen's Mystery Magazine* in recent years combining some of his own characters, but since he writes all the series, the stories required no collaboration. Married authors Marcia Muller and Bill Pronzini brought their detectives together for a few short stories and a novel as well.

In the early stories (there would be six in all) Rice and Palmer shared the ideas and the writing of the pieces. Palmer would relate later that the two never fought about the stories. Working as she had with Cleve Cartmill, Palmer wrote the first draft. Rice edited and made suggestions. As Rice's drinking continued, her contribution dropped off to consist mainly of ideas for plots and dialogue. Since two of the stories appeared years after Rice's death without a noticeable difference in style, readers deduced Palmer had been doing most of the actual writing. Palmer remembers talking to Rice about the series, "She always allowed me complete leeway with her beloved Malone, perhaps because of a feeling she expressed in a letter I still have: 'You know, Stu, if you weren't so tall and if you had a law degree, you'd be Malone. . .' . . . I felt flattered."[12]

The first story in this series was entitled "Loco Motive" and published as "Once Upon a Train." Rice wrote part of the first draft for this story. The story could be pure Craig Rice with only a few exceptions.

No orphans or abandoned children appear in the story. Rice had made her fortune on the travails of characters with no parents, and yet none grace the pages of "Loco Motive." Also, a grudging attitude to Withers exists, which could only have come from an author who didn't care for his creation. The attention to detail and name brand products is also new, with mentions of toiletries like Chanel, and designer ties. Other than that, the malapropisms, witty banter, and rye all make an appearance.

Malone wants his fee after exonerating his client, Steve Larsen, of charges of embezzlement. After hearing from one of the guests at the celebration party that his client has taken the Super-Century to New York City, Malone travels on the same train to find Larsen. He encounters Miss Hildegarde Withers, heading back to New York from a funeral. "She was a tall, angular person who somehow suggested a fairly well-dressed scarecrow. Her face seemed faintly familiar, and Malone wondered if they'd met before. Then he decided that she reminded him of a three-year-old who had winked at him in the paddock at Washington Park one Saturday and then run out of the money.

"'Are you really the John J. Malone?' She smiled.

"'. . . Are you on a case?'

"'Working my way through the second bottle,' he muttered." [13]

Larsen shows up dead and undressed in Miss Withers's compartment, and the duo hides his body from the people searching the cars for him. Call the denouement nepotism from Palmer, but Withers solves the case by realizing that Larsen had disguised himself as a sailor on the train. Malone receives a reward for finding the embezzled money, and the pair shares a nice dinner in Hildegarde's Manhattan apartment to celebrate their success and the start of a profitable partnership.

By late summer, more money problems strained the DeMott household to the breaking point. Rice applied to her old friend again. This time, Guymon owed a sizable chunk to the IRS himself and couldn't help them out. DeMott ended up borrowing $500 from his parents, which caused a huge fight between the couple. Several checks bounced and tempers flared. Rice had reached her fill of not having enough money.

The shadow of Larry Lipton hovered over their marriage, with Rice trying to adjust to the monetary situation. Lipton married Nettie

Brooks, his long-time secretary, at about this time. Brooks had been Lipton's secretary for many years (including the years when Rice was paying her salary). Lipton enjoyed having a non-writing spouse who provided no competition for the limelight. He and Brooks moved to the Venice Beach area, where Lipton continued to write. He wrote mostly poetry, and hung out in coffee shops, becoming one of the early Beat Poets. He spent a great deal of time in the company of Ginsberg and Kerouac. In typical Lipton fashion, he prided himself on butting heads with Kerouac about many things in the movement.

DeMott left Rice again, and she slipped into a deep depression. When she chose to end a relationship, Rice suffered no ill effects; however, if the spouse left Rice, she went into the depressive cycle of her bipolar nature. She had no tolerance for suffering rejection by the man she loved and spiraled downward whenever a break-up occurred. DeMott's departure stung.

Ironically, Rice filed for divorce, yet subsequently collapsed under the strain. First, she called DeMott from a Santa Monica hotel room, threatening to kill herself. When the police arrived, they found her with a bottle of whiskey and a large quantity of sleeping pills. Although she hadn't taken any of the medication, Los Angeles General Hospital admitted her for psychiatric observation.

After Rice told a judge that she had no intention of killing herself and only wanted to reconcile with her husband, the court released her. Less than a week later, Nan Rice found her unconscious at her home, and took her to Santa Monica Hospital. Rice remained in a coma for two days after taking some sort of sedatives. The doctors recognized the signs of depression and alcoholism, but felt that she was beyond help at this point. The years of alcohol abuse began to take their toll on her body.

Sadly, Rice had written a story on faked suicide called "Good-bye, Good-bye" only two years before. The story deals with singer Doris Dawn, who apparently tried to take her life three times. Malone intervenes, believing the girl's story that someone wants her dead. Doris's mother had killed herself over a lost love who had disappeared mysteriously from her life, and left a convoluted will to provide for her daughter and the man who had deserted her.

When Malone saw the young, beautiful singer on the ledge,

"There was a lump of ice where his stomach had been just a little while ago. Life was so wonderful, even with the remains of yesterday's warmed-over hangover, even with only five bucks in your pants . . ."[14] Malone realizes that the girl suffers from a fear of heights and doesn't plan on jumping. He takes the time to save her when the psychiatrist, minister, and police can't.

After the body of Doris' stepfather is found, Malone moves fast to rescue Doris from another "suicide" attempt. The real killer dies in a shoot-out, and Doris is saved. The tone of the piece has a "life should go on" feel. Rice wrote this story before her break-up with DeMott and the discovery of the unpaid taxes. The story won third place in the annual *Ellery Queen Mystery Magazine* awards for 1945.

While Rice's personal drama unfolded, changes took place in the radio and movie arenas. *The Amazing Mr. Malone*, with Gene Raymond now playing the title role, aired again. The series would run a year before it went off the air for a second and final time. United Artists picked up the option on *The Lucky Stiff* and decided to film it. Unlike the earlier films that Rice had been so involved in, she barely noticed this film and the lack of input shows. The Justuses disappeared from the plot and Brian Donlevy starred as Malone.

In November 1949, Rice was committed to Camarillo State Hospital for chronic alcoholism. Rice wouldn't go willingly. She had to be forced into a detox program there. Nancy Atwill had to petition the court to admit her mother for an indefinite period of time. The wire services picked up photos of Rice snarling at the photographers from behind bars. The shots are a startling contrast to her cover pose. Even at this point, the author couldn't stop doing publicity. *Time* made notes on the case, but chose not to publish them. Rice's dramatic downfall was too drastic even for their purposes.

The promotion backfired this time. Her behavior shocked and frightened many of her colleagues and friends. Guymon wrote to the hospital and Rice, offering his assistance. Instead of Rice, a nurse replied, assuring him that everything possible was being done for the mystery writer. Many of Rice's colleagues were embarrassed or ashamed, and lost track of the writer at this time.

CHAPTER N I N E

"It appears that she has had five legal last names but none of them is Rice"

The time at Camarillo State Hospital didn't help Rice's alcoholism because she couldn't admit that she had a drinking problem. Nancy Atwill remembers visiting Rice at the hospital, where she had the nurses captivated with her laughter and stories. The author charmed the other patients, glibly informing them that she had committed herself to the institution to collect information on a book she planned to write exposing the treatment of mental patients. The other resident patients treated her like royalty, impressed by the famous author in their midst.

The doctors didn't diagnose the bipolar disorder while Rice resided at the hospital as a patient. The most noticeable symptom of her condition was the addiction to alcohol. Since the doctors saw this, and Rice's family shared a long-standing drinking problem, the doctors sought to treat the alcoholism.

Since she stayed at Camarillo for only a short period of time, she didn't have an opportunity to display the full range of emotions that are needed for a successful diagnosis. Having been left by DeMott, she sank into a deep depression and exhibited no signs of her usual manic behavior. Because of the length of time spent in mania or melancholy, on average the diagnosis for bipolarity takes eight years. Rice was only at the facility for a matter of months. Especially in the late 1940s, bipolarity and depression were often not recognized, seen more as a matter of personal weakness than mental illness. Even so, studies have shown a link between bipolarity and creativity. In many cases, what is considered eccentric or bizarre behavior is also seen as being artistic. Writers like F. Scott Fitzgerald and Ernest Hemingway also suffered from bipolarity that remained untreated in their lifetimes.

Rice realized what she was up against in the facility. She didn't want to be at Camarillo, so she turned on the charm. She told the staff the same types of outlandish stories that she had shared with *Time* magazine. The nurses were soon catering to her, and the doctors found her to be enjoyable company compared to some of the more demanding patients they treated. Rice made it seem as if her problems stemmed only from the recent spate of bad luck she'd suffered in love. The years of hidden drinking served her well, as no record of a long-term pattern existed in her medical history.

The only treatments for manic-depression at the time of Rice's stay at Camarillo were lobotomies and ECT (electroconvulsive therapy). Even if Rice had been diagnosed correctly, the remedies might have destroyed any chance she had for continuing as a writer. Her books and the mystery world were one of Rice's main sources of self-identification. Would she or her family have opted to undergo these therapies if the result would have been an impaired person who had lost her ability to write? Doctors would be hard pressed to trim away the manic cycles of Rice's illness without cutting the creativity that added so much to her life (and the lives of her readers).

While bipolar disorder can be controlled chemically today, psychiatry had not advanced to that point in the late 1940s.

Doctors didn't prescribe lithium as a medication in the treatment of manic depression until the early 1960s. Lithium had been identified as a potential treatment of manic-depression as far back as the late 1950s; however, there was little commercial potential in using an element (lithium). Hence, the treatment did not get much press or consideration until the early 1970s. So, Rice had few options from the mental health profession to her problem. As a result, since she was left untreated for the root cause of her problems, she began to drink heavily almost as soon as she left the hospital.

In 1950, while living at the mental institution, Rice met her fourth husband (fifth by her own count), Paul Bishop. Proximity and sympathy seemed to be the major attractions, not a good combination when meeting in a mental health facility. Bishop left Camarillo prior to Rice, but she called him as soon as she was released. The relationship was volatile from the start. Rice had to call police on one of his first visits to her home, when he refused to leave. The refusal led to Bishop's arrest and return to the psychiatric ward.

Not much remained of the life she had known before the tax disaster, her last marriage, and suicide attempt. She had no home, no money, and few contacts. DeMott had moved away. Rice felt alone. Her dreams for happiness with a man had faded away again, and no *Time* cover could fill the void in her life.

At this vulnerable time, Rice and Bishop started corresponding and made short visits to each other. Bishop was a tall, dark-haired man with glasses and a mustache. Rice didn't notice his outbursts or violent mood swings; she either chose to ignore them or was too drunk to spot someone else's problems. His actions alarmed the people who knew Rice. Bishop demonstrated bizarre, anti-social behaviors, hiding in the closets when people came over. At other times, he would lash out at anything around him. Cursing, throwing things, and physical abuse became part of the household rituals.

However, he did treat Rice well at times, acting as a nurse during one of her increasingly severe eye attacks. Alone with this woman he didn't seem quite so strange. Like the rest of her husbands, Bishop called himself a writer. He claimed to have been a proofreader for Encyclopedia Britannica, and a short story writer.

After a short courtship, Rice and Bishop decided to elope to

Mexico. They went to Chihuahua and married. With Bishop's presence in her life, Rice lost her suicidal feelings from the divorce. The ink had barely dried on the DeMott divorce papers and her lawyers cautioned her to wait before remarrying or risk committing bigamy. Ignoring their legal advice, she married Bishop anyhow. Even with a new spouse, the drinking continued. Rice couldn't put words to paper in her current state. That meant she had no means to support herself or this husband.

As he had been with Larry Lipton, Stuart Palmer remained unimpressed with Rice's latest choice in husbands. "Stu ... met him at a very bad time, when Bishop had thrown his sacroiliac for a loss and was down at my beach cottage, unable to get up on his feet, and cross as a bear. We are both hot-tempered, which resulted in a terrific lovers' quarrel and a lot of very bad newspaper publicity."[1]

Rice's publicity of late had been thoroughly negative; the snarling face behind bars, the suicide attempts, and now the domestic disputes with Bishop. Former fans couldn't understand the downhill spiral of their favorite author, the humorous writer they had seen as a domestic role model (a supermom character) in *Home Sweet Homicide*. As a minor celebrity, Rice's exploits made the newspapers in whatever town they took up residence.

The couple decided to move to Mexico, and lived in a small hotel there. Rice sent for Nan Rice to come stay with them and began picking out furniture for a home. This was not a desire for moral support from her adoptive mother. Nan Rice was needed to pay the bills. As Rice's guardian, she managed Rice's financial affairs, which had been badly mangled by Rice and Lipton. As always, Rice started hitting up her old friend, Ned Guymon, for a few available dollars. Guymon loaned her $150 when she first arrived in Chihuahua, but declined further requests for help. When she bounced a check that had been signed by Nan Rice as her guardian, Guymon lost all hope of salvaging his friendship with Rice. "I can find no excuse for such a check to be written without funds to cover it and I blame Mrs. Rice and the U.S. Fidelity and Guarantee Company for so doing. The District Attorney's office here informs me that in their opinion I have grounds for a civil suit."[2] Guymon had suffered setbacks in his own business and showed little sympathy for Rice's continuing financial mismanagement. His financial advice to Rice went unheeded as her drinking worsened.

Bishop didn't have steady employment either. He professed to be a writer, but he had a union card from a machinists organization. In an unintended irony, Rice got marital advice from ex-husband, Larry Lipton. "As for Bishop, whom you mention in your wire, if you don't love him any more shake him off if he tried to work you for money. Nobody has a right to live on another person's labor without working. Let him do some work of his own and he won't have to bother you again."[3]

Bishop's reasons for being at Camarillo became obvious to his bride within a few weeks of moving to Mexico. Bishop took an overdose of sleeping tablets after a fight with Rice regarding a book review. He severely beat a neighbor's dog on a public street and police arrested him. The dog wasn't the only one to feel Bishop's wrath. He repeatedly beat Rice. In the many physical disputes, he dislocated her right shoulder and cracked her hip. Due to poor medical care in the backward country, she developed a limp trying to recover from the beatings. Rice didn't have money to consult a specialist. Instead, she used alcohol to dull the pain.

Yet, like many abused spouses, she refused to sign a complaint against him, especially given the state of Mexican jails. Rice couldn't bring herself to confine him to the inhumane conditions of the prisons. Also, holding on to a man was paramount to her. Bishop could not control his violence. Within a few weeks, they separated. Rice found herself in a foreign land with no cash and wired her friends for a few dollars to return home. By July, Rice decided that she had suffered enough. In all, only nine months had elapsed since the time she had been admitted to Camarillo.

However, leaving Bishop turned out to be more difficult than Rice planned. After she returned to Santa Monica, Rice learned that Bishop had followed her to the States, issuing death threats to her and Nan Rice. Upon finally investigating her husband's background, Rice discovered that his doctors had diagnosed Paul as a violent schizophrenic who should never have been released from Camarillo. The recommended treatment for Bishop was electric shock therapy or possibly a lobotomy, the standard therapies at the time for most mental conditions, including Rice's own. Terrified of what Bishop might do, Rice left her house to live with a friend. She kept a low profile and couldn't afford the publicity of publishing any work.

As in the stalking cases of today's headlines, the police couldn't do much to stop Rice's husband until he actually committed a crime in California. The beatings and violence in Mexico fell outside of the United States' jurisdiction. Rice's visits to the Santa Monica police and the state police produced no action. His doctors couldn't recommit Bishop to the hospital until the police arrested him, and the police couldn't arrest him without some proof of a crime. Rice found herself trapped in a vicious bureaucratic cycle.

With typical aplomb, Rice decided to write about the experience. Other than a few short stories, she had not written a word since her break-up with DeMott and she had a ready idea to work with. She planned a non-fiction article on being stalked. Although she contacted *Colliers* about the article, her efforts never got past the plot stage.

One short story Rice published during this period was "Good-Bye Forever," referencing a piece of music that supposedly brought bad luck to whoever recorded the song. Rice took the reader back to the recording studio milieu, a setting she hadn't used since *The Corpse Steps Out*. Once again, she vividly portrayed the radio setting and the people involved with it. In the story, Malone picks up a fee for protecting Larry Lee and his band from harm when Lee surreptitiously adds a few bars from the malevolent melody to a current composition. Malone, at one of his lowest career points, owes three months back rent and is in debt to everyone. Clearly, the author took her character with her on the downhill slide. The little lawyer was on his last dollar without much chance of a fee.

One of the few short stories where the emphasis doesn't lie on parentage, "Good-Bye Forever" concentrates instead on marital relations. Almost everyone in the story has secretly married another character, or quietly plans to divorce and remarry. When the clarinet player, the clandestine husband of the press agent, dies from poisoning, the reader can easily suspect (as does Malone) that the motive for the crime was not the playing of "Good-Bye Forever," but love.

The authorship of the Withers-Malone stories became clear when the second story featuring the two detectives appeared shortly after Rice's stay at Camarillo. "Cherchez la Frame" appeared in 1951 in *Ellery Queen's Mystery Magazine*. The story takes Malone to Los Angeles with Maggie and Withers. Palmer wasn't familiar with Chicago the way Rice was, so he moved the characters closer to his LA home. In the story, Malone has been hired to look for the long-lost love of Joe Vastrelli, a Chicago mob boss. When Nina LaCosta and another woman turn up strangled with Malone's brightly colored neckties, the Los Angeles police arrest him for the crimes. Hildegarde Withers comes to the rescue and solves the case through some rather unscrupulous means.

Palmer told Ned Guymon, "Fred [Dannay] wrote to me the other day, desperate [sic] for a Withers-Malone story and promising that I could write it alone, edit it alone, and that Rice would only get half the money. There seems to be something wrong with that too, though I can't put my finger on it. Anyway there is no question of her or any current husband having the last word on the final version."[4] By this time, Rice's writing was virtually non-existent. Her frequent moves and itinerant lifestyle didn't even allow her to carry a typewriter with her. When she did manage to have a typewriter, she frequently pawned it to buy booze or to pay her way out of a jam.

The Withers-Malone series begins to show Palmer's touch with this story. Malone's wardrobe is described in detail, "His suit was by Finchley, shirt by Brooks Brothers, but his tie was out of this or any world."[5] Rice had never bothered to dress Malone in any detail except for the occasional rumpled suits and neckties over his shoulder. The reader found credibility stretched by having different authors write about the same protagonist, because the same Malone that was three months behind in his rent couldn't shop at Brooks Brothers.

Maggie received a much bigger part in this series than the straight Malone short stories. Withers takes the secretary under her wing, and the two conspire for and against Malone depending on the circumstances. One of the first occasions Maggie appeared outside of the office, and certainly in her most verbose outing, she tells the whole story of Malone's involvement in the case to the schoolteacher, who wastes no time in jumping in the middle of things.

The Withers-Malone stories proved wildly popular with the readers of *Ellery Queen's Mystery Magazine* and MGM decided to make a film loosely based on the first story, "Once Upon a Train." The film changed the title to Mrs. O'Malley and Mr. Malone, with the Hildegarde Withers character being renamed O'Malley for the film, starring James Whitmore as Malone and Marjorie Main, most widely known as Ma Kettle, as the Withers-O'Malley character. The second story in the series was optioned by MGM, but the studio chose not to film it.

The film helped Rice on several levels. First, the money from the option and film allowed her to repay her debts to the government and take control of her finances again. Also, in order to sign the contracts for the movie deal Rice's guardianship (which had been invoked at the time of her commitment to Camarillo Hospital) had to be rescinded. Legally restored to mental competency, Rice no longer relied on Nan Rice for access to her money. The results of the legal paperwork were horrendous. She had no enforced budget and no watchdog over her money. No one could rein her in after this point.

Soon after she was restored to competency, Rice was sued again. Lewis Herman brought civil action against Rice for $5000. He claimed that Rice had promised him half of any advance that she received from *Innocent Bystander*. He had revised and polished the book prior to publication. Rice had changed the name of the book from *Murder-Go-Round*, and had neglected to pay him for his services.

Bishop tried to threaten Nan Rice, and had a bench warrant issued for his arrest when he failed to appear to face the charges. After the police captured Bishop and sent him back to the mental institution, Rice paid the costs involved to keep Bishop in a private institution. After her meager funds ran out, she claimed that their marriage was invalid and had him moved to Camarillo again. She and Nan Rice continued to live in a small boarding house together, on social security and whatever Rice could scrape together from friends and her agent.

Rice used some of the money to invest as part-owner of a liquor store and apartment building, not a wise choice for an alcoholic. Rice wasted no time in drinking her way through the inventory. The house provided her a place to stay at half rent, and she continued her downhill slide on the few profits she received from the other owners.

When Camarillo released Rice's husband again, the couple reconciled. Rice clung to the hope of maintaining a relationship with him. Within weeks, Bishop sent money for Rice to join him in New Mexico.

They took up residence in Albuquerque, but left in early 1951 after a fight with the landlord. The couple drank heavily, hosting parties for people they barely knew. The noise and the failure to pay rent caused problems with the landlord. Within a few weeks, they split up again and took separate routes to Santa Fe. Along the way, Rice lost over three hundred dollars in cash through negligence. She paid her cab fair to a motel in Santa Fe with a $100 bill and didn't bother to wait for change, or had it stolen from her, depending on who told the story. That news made the local papers. By the time she met up with her husband in Santa Fe, Rice had lost all her money.

The event made the front page of the Santa Fe papers. Both Rice and Bishop contacted the police about their missing spouse and the loss of several hundred dollars. She claimed to have been robbed, even though the cabby explained the $100 fare and tip. Along the way, Rice misplaced her purse and the police were contacted about that incident as well. She made it seem as if the purse had been stolen, not lost due to drunkenness. The couple quickly became a nuisance to the officials. Their problems couldn't stay private.

After only about ten weeks, the Bishops separated again in a particularly ugly split. More fights, more publicity. Rice moved into a separate hotel in Santa Fe. Bishop advertised in the newspaper that he would no longer be responsible for Rice's debts. The next day, Bishop signed a police complaint against Rice for entering his apartment through the bedroom window in order to steal his money and keys. After she was arrested and sentenced to thirty days in jail for drunkenness, the prison doctors transferred Rice to a local hospital for observation. Bishop left the area, and Rice's life, at this point. By the time Rice was released from jail, Bishop had vanished. Though he would contact her from time to time for money in the future, they never attempted another reconciliation.

Rice never forgave Bishop for this final desertion. This was her third split in only four years, and Rice continued to spiral downward from this point. Just before her death, Rice went back to Mexico in order to file for divorce from Bishop. The grounds for the divorce were desertion. She despised him to her dying day and actually added a codicil to her will that excluded him from ever making a claim against her estate.

CHAPTER TEN

"No popular magazine would dream of buying a story in which as a matter of course enough liquor is drunk to float a distillery."

With no home in California and no significant male relationship, Rice had nothing to hold her to the West Coast. In January 1952, Rice moved to New York City to revive her flagging career. With the exception of a few short stories, she had not written anything publishable in several years, nor completed a novel in almost four years. The quality of her stories had suffered as she tried to rush them to make a fast sale without the luxury of polishing or a rewrite. Despite her pleas for cash, Tony Boucher, who edited True Crime Detective at that time as well as writing mystery reviews, returned several of her stories for being poorly written. Her work had slid into an amateurish, sloppy style, brought on in large part by her drinking. A story circulated that Rice called her editor at Simon & Schuster, Lee Wright, asking if she had read her latest manuscript and Lee replied, "Yes, I did. Have you?" Tales like this did little to help Rice's attempts at a comeback. By this point, the nation knew of Rice's troubles. The same publicity machine she used to get notice didn't stop when things went bad.

In New York City, Rice took any writing job she could find to make ends meet. Going to interview a Spanish musician at the old St. Nicholas arena, Rice received incorrect instructions on how to find the guitar player. "So I followed directions — came to the first door on my right and opened it, expecting to step into a lighted office and on a level floor — and stepped down twenty feet of concrete stairs into the basement."[1] Rice landed on her left side and her arm. She spent three weeks in the hospital trying to recuperate, and was left with a plaster cast encasing her left arm. The story made the headlines of several papers, and did nothing to restore Rice's reputation. The papers had exaggerated the extent of her injuries, and Rice did nothing to disavow the claims.

The doctors ended up placing a steel plate in her upper left arm, and performed several operations, which required months of casts. The surgery made it difficult for her to type or accomplish any work. Rice's agent tried to assist her in making money to pay the bills. She suggested an omnibus of Rice's crime reporting to Lee Wright. Simon & Schuster compiled and published a series of her true crime articles as *45 Murderers*.

The attempted comeback was short-lived. Lipton alleged that he had written most of the articles and sued for a part of the royalties. Considering that Rice was fired from her position at Hearst because of the poor quality of the true crime work, Lipton laid claim to mediocrity. Despite the lawsuit, many of the stories had been written following their initial separation. After a long court battle, the judge awarded him sixty percent of all royalties from the book. Lipton had to sign the contracts for the works, and was pleased by the sale of the television and radio rights. Rice was not much better off financially for the effort.

Lipton's motivation in suing was more vanity than monetary. He'd never forgiven Rice for surpassing him in fame, especially with her *Time* cover. By saying the work was his, he was telling the world that her fame was due him as well. By the time Rice died, her literary agent had lost contact with Lipton and didn't know how to pay royalties

from *Murderers* to him. Lipton made no effort to keep in touch or claim
the cash from Rice's work. He simply wanted to gain recognition from
his famous ex-wife, and maintain some form of control over her.
Lipton's fame rested solely in its proximity to others.

The collection, *45 Murderers*, a rather disjointed affair, contained
forty-five short pieces on murders from around the country. The only
common thread running through all the features was that the cases
involved murders, and most had a connection to Southern California.
Rice's one-time secretary, Peggy O'Leary, had researched some of the
crimes for *The Los Angeles Murders*. Other cases had caught Rice's
attention via the newspapers, and the rest resulted of her true-crime
features in the newspapers and the short-lived *Craig Rice Crime Digest*.

Rice could vary her style with the type of work. She'd shown that
with the Venning series. Rice wrote these crime stories with a gossipy
feel. The hook would either be a dramatic moment in the case or the
type of supposition, which couldn't fail to intrigue the reader. The
piece, "Girl Loses Boy", begins this way: "It began like a story any
Hollywood studio would have jumped at. Boy meets girl. Wartime
romance. Beautiful young red-haired Irish nurse, and handsome
young American. A romantic and definitely photogenic meeting —

"Marriage, and a baby.

"But this story ended in tragedy. The last of the many photographs taken of Bridget Waters showed her kissing her baby goodbye,
after being sentenced to prison. The handsome young American husband was dead."[2]

Each story covers an unusual crime, ranging from white slavery
to mutilations. Attesting to Rice's enthusiasm for her work, the pieces
have been reprinted repeatedly. Typically, true crime cases contain an
element of timeliness which dates the story quickly. However, the stories in *45 Murderers* have withstood time.

As with the Heirens case, when she received so much publicity
and denunciation, Rice often sought to inject her own theories about
the killer or the motive. In "The Black Dahlia Case," the same case
made famous by James Ellroy's book, Rice wrote about a young woman
found cut in half by an unknown killer. Rice supposed, "It was not a
crime of sudden passion, perpetrated by a person of brief acquaintance
with the victim, and the job of disposing of the body was not a sudden

impulsive one. Investigation will finally reveal . . . that the murderer of The Black Dahlia was someone who had long carried a grudge against the unfortunate girl."[3] As she had been in the Heirens case, Rice guessed wrong on this case. She said that one day the case would be marked closed.

Given her place in the mystery community of Southern California, Rice knew a variety of law enforcement officers and spoke to them when writing the stories that went into the collection. Rice readily bandied about the names of police officials and criminologists in her stories to support her theories, and added details to the cases to which the public didn't yet have access.

When Rice moved to New York to help her career, she left her family behind in California. Rice missed the birth of her third grandchild when Nancy Atwill gave birth in early January, to another girl, named Christine. The family had no way of contacting the author. She moved so frequently that she didn't bother to notify anyone of her where-abouts. Forwarding addresses were worthless.

However, family problems didn't end with Rice's departure. Shortly after Christine's birth, Nan Rice had a debilitating stroke and was hospitalized. She had been living in a small apartment by herself, but the doctors told Nancy Atwill that Mrs. Rice could no longer take care of herself. Nan Rice moved in with Nancy and Joe Atwill, and their growing brood. After lasting only a few more weeks, Nan Rice passed away. No one could locate Rice for the funeral, and she didn't learn of her adoptive mother's death for some time. In New York, Rice went from man to man and stayed in flophouses between relationships. The move had done nothing to stabilize her life. When the author later learned of the death, she was upset and carried on. However, she had caused Nan Rice considerable grief in her last years, moving the elder-ly woman across Southern California and Mexico for her own purpos-es.

While Rice lived in New York, her daughter, Iris, married a friend of her Uncle Christopher, a very artistic man fifteen years her senior. Matthew Adams, a painter and interpreter in the Army, had been born a British colonial in Nagasaki, Japan. Iris would later recount that she had fallen in love with his deep, sonorous voice and could not resist his proposal. Iris's wedded bliss lasted no longer than her mother's had.

The couple divorced in less than a year. While living in Los Angeles, Iris began working at KABC-TV as a proofreader. She received a promotion to the operations department, where she scheduled the day's shows.

Adding to the tumultuous time, Lipton sued for $11,000 that he claimed Rice owed him from the property settlement of their divorce. Lipton now contended that he had co-authored the works by "Craig Rice", a far step up from bouncing around ideas and the occasional revision. "I am doing just that when I give you permission to use my own work, done under our joint authorship and under the name of Craig Rice, to publish and collect royalties on."[4] This time Rice chose to fight, and the battle raged on in court for months. Although he published a book of poetry during this time, Lipton hadn't written a book in the years since his divorce from Rice. He relied on the royalties from Rice's work and on his wife Nettie (who worked at UCLA as a secretary) for support. Lipton remained the same contentious person he'd always been, only now he vented it on different people.

He became very involved with the Beat Poets and wrote poetry during the 1950s, although he didn't fit in well with the Venice Beach crowd where he lived. Keeping the same leftist leanings he had while married to Rice, he argued bitterly with Jack Kerouac over politics. Kerouac was dismissive of Lipton (who was in his mid-50s by this time). Lipton published a book in the late 1950s called *The Holy Barbarians* that made use of his relationships with many of the same poets. Kerouac was annoyed by Lipton, and frequently ridiculed him in letters. As the careers of some of the Beat poets took off, Lipton was once again left behind.

Lipton's lawsuit wasn't the only day in court for Rice. To help defray some of the hospital and doctor bills from her debilitating accident, Rice found a lawyer who encouraged her to sue the arena for $150,000. Since she had been rendered unable to type by the accident, it resulted in a loss of income that she wanted to recover. The guard who had given her the instructions that led to her mishap had recently started his job, and was confused about the layout of the arena. The case was weakened because Rice was drunk at the time and most likely misunderstood his directions.

Still in casts, Rice met another man, Arthur Neale, in New York City. He installed the invalid author at his mother's house. Rice paid a minimal rent to be nursed while she recovered. She still had her arm in plaster and found typing difficult at best. She re-initiated contact with Ned Guymon now that her prospects for money had improved. Her relatively brief letters didn't request any assistance from her rich friend (for which he was grateful). She suffered from bouts of fever that she attributed to malaria that she'd picked up in Mexico while she was with Bishop. Rice suffered a few more hospital stays before she could move out on her own. Of course, the police were never far behind, and one of Rice's guests at a party was arrested for assaulting Neale.

Rice indicated to Guymon that she planned to marry her latest flame in New York, but in early May 1952, they broke up and Rice moved into the Hotel Somerset on 47th Street, where she and Lipton had spent time when they traveled to New York City. A desk clerk found the author one night, unconscious from an overdose of sleeping pills. Rice had called the front desk and threatened to jump out of the hotel room window, despondent over this latest break-up. Hospitalized at Bellevue for several days, Rice was released and found another Times Square hotel.

In late 1952, Rice switched literary agents. The Ann Watkins agency primarily handled novel length works, which Rice had not produced in years. The author went to the Scott Meredith Agency, where Evan Hunter (who would go on to literary fame, both under his own name and the pseudonym Ed McBain) worked as an executive editor.

"The receptionist told me, Craig Rice is here and I went in to Scott and I said, 'Craig Rice is here. Who's Craig Rice? — because I had never heard of him.' I went out and talked to her and she was drunk and abused. She opened her blouse and showed me the bruises on her shoulders and above her breasts. I brought her into him [Scott Meredith] and he talked to her for awhile and he asked her to write a story for *Manhunt* and he said we would pay her up front, but she had to come to the office everyday and write it. *Manhunt* magazine was pretty big at the time and it was sort of an open secret that the agency was putting it together.

"We were paying her for the stories up front [before publication], but we would pay her at the end of the day. I think the deal was we would pay her when she finished the story, because we were not at all sure that she wouldn't take the money and blow it on booze."[5]

The worry about her alcoholism proved well founded. Rice continued to drink constantly and heavily. She attended the monthly MWA
meetings so intoxicated that the other members escorted her home.
Many of the members recall these events with some embarrassment.
Rice was a very lonely woman at this time, and wanted a man to make
her happy. She would proposition men at the MWA meetings, either
outright or by asking for help in getting home. Once at her place, she
would try to seduce her escort. The men of the early 1950s were not
ready for a sexually liberated, middle-aged woman, albeit a drunk one,
and were aghast at the forthrightness of Rice's behavior.

Ironically, the sexism of the period etched Rice's behavior into
the minds of the MWA attendees. Several of the male authors drank
excessively and had affairs. John Dickson Carr was a heavy drinker and
womanizer; however, Rice's behavior became inextricably linked with
her body of work. Hammett and Chandler would be judged on the
basis of their works alone.

Rice's drinking also brought out the worst in other people. Fights
erupted around her and with her during her stay in New York. On at
least one occasion, she duked it out with one of the male writers at an
MWA meeting. Her drinking made her coarse and belligerent. Other
fights between amorous rivals happened at her apartment and various
parties in New York City, adding to the bruises and beatings she had
taken. Still not healed from her fall, Rice's body continued to be abused
by men and by alcohol.

Stemming from her limited capabilities in the early 1950s, questions have arisen over the authorship of the short stories produced
during that period. The Scott Meredith Agency had a reputation in the
literary community for sometimes selling ghostwritten work for their
clients. Some of the later Ellery Queen novels fell into this category,
with one member of the Queen writing team approving the story idea
and ghostwriter. In their work *Detective Fiction: A Collector's Guide*, John
Cooper and B. A. Pike significantly reduce the Rice canon of uncollected short stories. "It seems, there is a considerable problem of authen-
ticity . . . Detailed research is evidently needed. . . With many deletions
and a few additions, . . . [the] list reduced to thirty-six [from sixty-five]
'Craig Rice' stories and the single Michael Venning."[6]

With the evidence that Rice wrote under the supervision of the

Meredith agency while living in New York, the assumption can be made that Rice wrote many of the stories from this time period. During the writing of this biography, typewritten manuscripts of some of Rice's work from Rice's collection *45 Murderers* came to light at the home of one of Rice's grandchildren. While no tests were run, they appeared to have the same characteristics of Rice's letters to Ned Guymon and Fred Dannay. One of the questioned works, "The Murdered Magdalen", appeared in 1955 in *Mercury Mystery Book Magazine*. As evidenced by manuscripts possessed by the family, Rice most likely wrote the short stories from the New York time period. The probability that Lipton wrote them drops as well. More likely ghostwritten are some of the short works from the time period of 1954 to 1956 and the posthumous novel, *But the Doctor Died . . .*.

One of the first Malone stories written by Rice for her new agency was "The Murder of Mr. Malone." The story concerns Malone and Maggie in Los Angeles, looking into the death and will of an elderly woman who left everything to a young woman she had never met. When a man that Malone meets at an airport bar ends up dead with Malone's airline ticket, Maggie helps keep her boss under cover until the murderer can be revealed, and Malone has the rare opportunity of seeing his own funeral. Rice followed the same form she had in her other short work of not including the Justuses in the short stories, leaving the reader to wonder why his best friends, Jake and Helene, are missing from Malone's memorial service.

In writing (as with most creative skills), constant practice is needed to keep up talent. Rice had been out of practice for four years. This was not one of Rice's better Malone efforts. The story appears as if Rice had the idea for a novel and crammed the plot into a short story for quick money: it is a complicated tale with too many characters and not enough motivation.

In addition to the Justuses' absence, other details in the story don't ring true. Maggie had grown from one line per book to a more well-rounded character, and received a last name. She was christened Mary Margaret Gogarty for this story alone. Maggie seems to have become the super-secretary by predicting her boss's movements and plans, and helping him out. The work is more indicative of Palmer's version of Malone, with Maggie's involvement and the Los Angeles setting.

Rice also wrote a series of short shorts that appeared in a variety of magazines. The stories, including "The Dead Mr. Duck", "Motive", and ". . . And Be Merry," featured Malone, von Flanagan, and a psychiatrist evaluating a mystery. The works all end with a strange twist that leave the reader wondering about the mental health of all the characters. Rice's recent brushes with psychiatry showed in her material. Many of her later works would feature psychologists.

With each day spent in an office setting, the quality of Rice's material showed improvement. The stories were no longer first draft quality. The plot and characterizations worked. She took the time to polish her stories. Some of her old humor and form began to re-emerge.

In "The Tears of Evil", the reader can see Rice progress in her writing skills by working at her craft. Malone attends a small party to celebrate the fifteenth wedding anniversary of his friends, George and Kathy Weston. When George discovers Kathy brutally murdered at the party, Malone sets out to find a killer among the guests.

The tone of this story reminds the reader of Rice's previous novel, *Innocent Bystander*, with its gritty feel that Rice usually doesn't use in the Malone stories. The Westons were carnival employees who rode motorcycles in the mesh cage loop-the-loop, and who have now struck it rich in Chicago real estate. Kathy Weston's body is found nude, covered with a sheet by George when he finds her. This story comes closest to hard-boiled as Rice wrote. Without the usual wit and the malapropisms, "The Tears of Evil" is a straightforward detective story.

A personal triumph for Rice at this point was the sale of "Eyes Up in Moonlight," published as "Death in the Moonlight," the Melville Fairr story in which the victim died from sex. *Popular Detective* agreed with Fred Dannay, and Rice made concessions to the publisher by changing the last paragraphs to say that the victim died of happiness and not from too much sex. Rice was willing to compromise the ending for money at this point.

One of Rice's most anthologized works, "And The Birds Still Sing," was published by *Ellery Queen Mystery Magazine* in late 1952. The story, fast paced and funny, has Malone swapping clients' checks faster than he can cash them. When Mona Trent asks Malone to investigate a case, he happily obliges since he needs the cash again. However, before she can pay Malone a retainer, he finds her dead in her apartment. The police suspect Eddie Carter, Mona's ex-boyfriend and a jockey gone wrong, and Paul and Leonora Cartwright, Mona's current boyfriend and his wife.

One by one, as von Flanagan arrests the suspects, each retains the little lawyer. His troubles arise when the police release each potential client before he can cash the hefty retainer checks for defending them. Malone finally gets to the bottom of the case with some good deductive thinking and a solid use of the clues.

The story marks a return to the old Rice style and flair, with a Malone sharp and wise-cracking and full of compassion for the victim. Von Flanagan complains about his job, and Joe the Angel dispenses words of wisdom along with the drinks and the loans to his favorite client. Rice seemed to have hit her stride again during this short time.

Another story from the same period is "Life Can Be Horrible." The Scott Meredith Agency sold the best of the Rice stories to *Ellery Queen Mystery Magazine*, where Fred Dannay gladly bought his old friend's work. The rest of the stories appeared in the digest-sized mystery magazines like *Manhunt* — as this one did. Malone defends the two nephews of Joe the Angel for the murder of the husband of a female wrestler. Nadine Sapphire, the grappler in question, had hired the boys to steal $10,000 dollars from her husband. Malone quickly sends the pair out of town, a strategy he'll use again in the later *Knocked For A Loop*. He returns to the scene of the crime, where he finds the body missing and the money returned.

The story reminds the reader of some of Rice's novel-length plots, but in a short format the characters can't breathe, and the developing plot screams to a halt for the denouement. Her better stories have a manic quality, but in a controlled version that lets the reader enjoy the ride without being jerked around excessively.

"The End of Fear", another story from this period, is an attempt to synthesize Rice's two styles. The first part of the piece recounts the flight of Meri Adsmith from justice after the murder of two men known to her. The gritty style evokes *Innocent Bystander*, like many other of Rice's works from the period. Adsmith's path takes her to Chicago, where she enlists of the help of John J. Malone, and the second half of the story begins there. The last portion of the story has Malone at his best, avoiding the police and clearing an innocent woman.

"The End of Fear" represents one of the few Malone short works where Helene Justus appears. She helps Meri elude the police by assuming her place, so that Malone can hide the fugitive until he solves the case. With many of the later cases, Malone must go to Los Angeles, Santa Monica in this case, to solve the crime. The plot remains one of Rice's better ones from this era; however, the two styles require the reader to shift gears mid-story, which is rather disconcerting.

Rice's feeling of emotional disconnectedness comes through in "Quiet Day in the County Jail," the story of a young woman locked in protective custody, about to testify against a killer. The only woman in an all-male prison, Red, the only name given to the witness, is treated well by the other prisoners and wardens. The story contains only one scene with little plot, showing Red preparing to leave for the trial at which she may never testify.

"Quiet Day" leaves the reader vaguely uneasy with the feeling of emotional distance between the characters. The other inmates frequently talk about Red as if she isn't there, or in the past tense. The men's feelings of fear and sorrow are masked in song or jokes, or the small presents they give to her in the final pages of the piece. Rice's own feelings of being lost in a world of men and yet unconnected to them can be read between the lines.

Rice held to her belief that love can redeem someone, as she wrote about in "The Bells Are Ringing." The story has no mystery to the murder. because the shooting took place in a crowded police station. Malone locates the fugitive, and has to determine why John Drew shot the policeman who had brought him in on a minor charge. The little lawyer discovers that Drew was arrested on his way to his wedding to his sweetheart, a young woman with tuberculosis who is about to die. Malone helps the escapee get to his wedding and marry the bride before her death.

The story begins, "It isn't often that a man gets a chance to live a moment of his life over again and do the right thing where he had once done wrong. This is the story of a man who got such a chance, paid for it — with his life."[7] Rice added a hint of sentimentality to the fleeing suspect and barely mentioned the dying police officer. The story doesn't work well because the reader wonders why the wedding held more importance than a man's life.

Rice sought to improve her work as she wrote more. To combat claims that her gangsters lacked realism, "The Dead Undertaker" portrays a more serious underworld of Chicago for Rice. Local funeral parlors are being used to collect the names of the deceased so those names can be used to fill out voter rolls in elections. One of the undertakers decides to confess by passing a list of names to Malone during a parade through downtown Chicago. The man dies before he can forward the information to the little lawyer, and Malone sets himself up as the bait to catch the killer at the parade.

If the adage that your life flashes before your eyes before death holds true, Malone's literary life passes before him in this short story. Rice stuffs references to Hercules the bloodhound, Joshua Gumbril, and others in this story. Some of Rice's later short works contain more of a tie with the past through references to Malone's earlier legal feats. As Rice's work improved, the desire to tie her works together through odd quirks and references grew.

Rice also included some of Malone's unrecorded cases in these short stories. In a similar vein to the Holmes stories, she mentioned in passing "the jolly little man in the Hanson ax-murder cases on the South Side"[8] and the cases where the motive for murder was a teddy bear. Sadly, Rice didn't live long enough to record more of these missing Malone cases.

Despite the cash that Scott Meredith paid Rice, the problems and drinking didn't stop. She continued to float from man to man, trying to nurture a relationship. Her need for money to buy alcohol prevented her from beginning another novel.

At one point, Rice disappeared out on to the streets on New York, As Stuart Palmer wrote in a letter; "They are hunting for Craig Rice down Skid Row with a warrant to send her back to Camarillo. She hasn't picked up the mail at her former apartment for almost two months. I'm afraid she drinks."[9]

Back in Los Angeles, Rice's son, David Ferguson, was released from the Navy, and started attending UCLA for a degree in mathematics. While he was still in the Navy, he had met a young woman, Carolyn Baxter, during a visit to Big Bear. They married in October, 1953. David Ferguson worked at the university to support the family while he attended school.

Rice returned to California shortly before David Ferguson's discharge from the Navy. She continued to drink heavily and Nancy Atwill considered returning her mother to Camarillo for further treatment. Rice had found another beau in the meantime. The latest man in her life, Henri Maliverni, she introduced as her rich husband from Liechtenstein (or Luxembourg or Lithuania, depending on the audience), although in reality he was another unemployed writer. He was a fraud who was trying to take advantage of a well-known writer. Rice was always a sucker for a good story, even if it wasn't true. Many people assumed she was affluent. After all, she had been a nationally recognized author. Still, matrimony was out of the question. No records exist of a divorce from Bishop, and the string of men that Rice purported to marry makes the tales extremely unlikely. In her state, Rice didn't bother with the legalities or formalities of civil ceremonies.

By this time, her friends in mystery had reached their limit. Stuart Palmer wrote this to Ned Guymon: "The new husband was picked up in a bar and has not a sou to his name; he expects to wax fat on the income of a famous mystery author. He is above work. Four words omitted here by censor. I am more bored with that situation than you can believe . . . I guess I'll have to change my phone number again."[10]

CHAPTER ELEVEN

"it is doubtful whether she [Mary Randolph] will get to California to see her daughter. . ."

R ice found herself barely able to function physically by 1954. Only forty-six, Rice looked decades older than her chronological age. The physical abuse by her husbands, boyfriends, and suitors took their toll. The beatings meted out in Mexico by Paul Bishop had been the worst, though not the only. The less-than-adequate Mexican medical facilities had left her with a limp. Combined with the fall onto the concrete floor which had scarred her left side and left a plate in her arm, her body was damaged to a point where walking became a chore. She had gone untreated for most of the physical problems received in New York. When Rice admitted herself to a hospital for related ailments, the doctors diagnosed her as having nerve damage.

Confined to a wheelchair and unable to type, she took up residence at the Rancho Los Amigos, a long-term care facility for multiple sclerosis patients in Hondo, California. The doctors could not diagnose Rice's specific ailment, simply stating that she suffered from a severe shock to the central nervous system.

Rancho provided Rice with a room and several hours of physical therapy a day. The facility was established to treat patients with MS and polio, and Rice's symptoms mimicked those of multiple sclerosis. She had difficulty moving her joints and getting around. "Maybe Stu Palmer wrote you that I landed out here some six months ago, almost totally paralyzed. With grave predictions by learned doctors that while I would never walk or stand again, in a year I might be able to propell [sic] a wheel chair and use my hands 'a little', But with the added thought that if any place could help, it would be the Rancho. Well, as you can see, I'm using my hands again (can even tat!), I get everywhere in my chair - even play croquet and go square dancing do everything for myself including making my own bed, and I can walk quite a few steps on a therapist's arm! Another six months and I'll be good as new - or better, as, viewed from the read, my new walk is very much like that of Marilyn Monroe. Which just goes to prove, you can't keep a squirrel on the ground or a Rice in bed."[1]

Photographs taken at the time of her admittance to Rancho show her with braces on both arms, perpendicular to her side, trying to type. The photos of the manic comic writer reduced to hunt and peck is a sad sight. The woman from the *Time* cover was gone, replaced by a gaunt-faced, gray haired woman.

Palmer described her condition, "Now they think she will live, but she must stay there at least six months. They had to pull all her teeth, and then she had to get necrosis of the jawbone. Her hair, what is left of it, is bone-white. She is in a wheel-chair part of each afternoon but cannot phone or write a line or even sign her name. . ." Malnutrition, anemia, acute alcoholism, crippled arm...."[2]

In addition to the time in therapy, Rice spent a great deal of time talking with her neighbors and reading mysteries to them. Nancy Atwill recalls that many patients who knew Rice at the facility called her years later, to tell her how much support Rice had been to them at Rancho and expressing gratitude for the author's encouragement. Rice would push people to work their hardest to improve, and assisted them in any way possible. Given the prognosis of the other patients facing a painful death, Rice forgot about her own loneliness and concentrated on helping others. With her limited mobility, drinking became next to impossible at the medical facility.

The mind-numbing depression of the past few years had begun to lift. Therapists often advise their patients to help the less fortunate, which allows them to see their own problems in perspective. In living at the home for MS patients, Rice met multitudes of people who would not be improving or going home. She would heal. She'd be released. As Rice realized her own problems were minor in comparison, she felt more relaxed with herself and began to write again.

Even with the time on her hands, several months passed in which Rice could not write because of her illness. The Meredith agency didn't want the comeback started by Rice to end now. They hired ghostwriters to whip out Malone short stories and other short work to keep her name in the pulps. Unlike the later Queen efforts, the agency didn't negotiate with the ghostwriters to have the copyright under her name. Instead, a number of articles appeared with different names listed on the copyright statement.

Malcolm Koch wrote "The Little Knife That Wasn't There" in 1954. In the story, Malone hops a train to California for the unusual reason of seeing a bookie. He wakes to find himself heading east, with a strange cast of characters on the train. When a murder is committed by one of the passengers, Malone does some quick thinking and determines the murderer. The weapon has to be one of the most questionable and weirdest ever used to slit a throat: a woman's fingernail.

The story pales in comparison to the Palmer-Rice "Once Upon A Train." Although the story passes as a mystery with a questionable murder method, it definitely doesn't rank with Rice's best short fiction, lacking wisecracks and orphans in the plot. Surprisingly, Fred Dannay printed this story, although he should have been able to easily determine that Rice didn't write it.

Much better was Stuart Palmer's effort, "Autopsy and Eva" which appeared in *Ellery Queen's Mystery Magazine* in 1954. The third of the Palmer-Rice stories takes place again in California, outside Malone's familiar Chicago environs. The story concerns a young woman accused of murdering her war-veteran husband, who had just returned home from Korea. Withers decides that the girl is innocent, and takes her on as a project with Malone.

Again the little details that give away Palmer's authorship are there, with his word choices and stylistic changes. His previously mentioned attention to the description of Malone's wardrobe becomes a recurring aspect. Ironically, these details would be used by some of the people who wrote under the Rice name as if they had mimicked her style (and not Palmer's).

Palmer produced another story shortly after this entitled, "Rift in the Loot" which features Malone's first fee received in working with Hildegarde Withers. An ex-client turned escaped convict, Eddie "the Actor" Vance, coerces Malone into finding the missing loot from a bank robbery. When Malone and his reluctant sidekick, Miss Withers, go to pick up the cash, they find the dead body of Eddie's ex-girlfriend. They have to explain their presence to von Flanagan and solve the murder for him. The case wraps up at the Art Institute, where Malone turns over a murderer, the escaped convict and the cash. Palmer had no way of knowing that Rice's mother, Mary Randolph, had attended that same school fifty years before. Rice was not apt to speak of her. The story had none of the acrimony or jealousy that Rice would have injected to the place her mother loved so dearly.

This story marks the first appearance of one of Rice's non-detective characters in any work produced by someone other than the author. Von Flanagan doesn't fare as well in this story. He comes off only as a dumb cop with none of the "artist's soul inside a working stiff" mentality that Rice imbued him with. While Malone can be caricatured as bombast and booze, his wit and one-liners were relatively easy to replicate. The manic characteristics of a Jake or Helene, or the complaints of the policeman, proved more difficult and while exceptions exist, few others tried.

As Rice's creativity began to reassert itself, she started a new mystery series in the form of a short story, "Mrs. Schultz is Dead." The series featured a reporter from the *Gazette* named Winklehoff, who has a job at the paper for life, and Regan, the city editor who must motivate the lifer into writing the compelling stories he's capable of. Together with Tom Ward of the police department, they solve the mystery of a body found in the living room of a vacant house. Regan receives a phone call that announces Mrs. Schultz is dead. When they arrive to investigate, they find the body of a call girl, who they take for Mrs. Schultz. When the *Gazette* runs a story to that effect, Mr. Schultz announces that he isn't married; hence, the woman couldn't be his wife. The team must investigate the murder to keep the paper from lawsuits.

Too many similarities to her other series exist to mention all of them. As in all of her series, Rice uses orphans as her primary characters. In this instance, Mr. Schultz has a stepson with no living parents. The stepson brings the newspaper into the story to prove his stepfather guilty of murder, bringing in the ill-treated child motif again. In addition, the call girl died from alcohol-related illnesses, certainly an ironic touch for Rice. In addition to the ever-intoxicated Malone, Jake, and Helene, Rice included more minor characters with drinking problems in her later work.

This series consisted of two short stories, the other one being "The Man From Turner's Was Here." As with the Kuzak-Riggs novels, the readers wanted Malone-Justus stories, and didn't give the same level of enthusiasm to any other project.

Rice used some of the work she produced while writing at the Meredith Agency during this period. When Rice provided her favorite short story for the collection *My Best Murder Story*, she selected "The Last Man Alive," a short story written while in New York, but never published. Echoing her own fears of being without a relationship, Rice wrote about the piece in her introduction, "I tried to incorporate some of the unutterable fear which we all have—the fear of being the last man alive in the world."[3] The story starts out with a science fiction/fantasy feel in a world inhabited by only one person, but quickly develops into a routine murder investigation. Ned Godwin awakes in a room next to a dead man. He leaves the room, but finds no one in the hotel or on the street, giving the story its title. When he returns to the room, the police have arrived and arrest him for the murder of this man he had never met before. No series characters appear in the story and sadly, little of the fear that Rice referenced.

Scott Meredith placed the Malone stories as soon as they were written. "I'll See You in My Dreams" is the story of a man who dreams that he killed his wife and comes to Malone concerned that he might do the deed during his waking hours. Malone uses his extensive knowledge of blondes to solve the case, perhaps a first in mystery fiction.

The plot twist again uses Rice's device from *Having Wonderful Crime*. She enjoyed inserting the device in her works, sometimes with more success than others. Having read so many mysteries for her review column, Rice took a delight in modifying the old mystery clichés. "I'll See You in My Dreams," one of the lesser examples of her plot device, relies heavily on a slip of the tongue and a talkative killer. She corresponded with Fred Dannay on stories that included a guilty butler. She talked up the genre with the people at Rancho, and acted as an information source for favorite authors and good books.

Another dream story improved on the theme, "Beyond The Shadow of a Dream" which was published in 1955. The title, derived from Keats's "Endymion," points to a more lucid Rice, who extracted ideas from her poetry background. Again the story is one of a man who dreams murders, but the similarity ends there. The man has dreamed of killing his psychiatrist, and the doctor pays a visit to Malone. When the psychiatrist turns up dead, Malone solves the case through logical deduction and use of conversation. The solution is a much more satisfying one, with Malone getting the girl as well.

In his introduction, Fred Dannay includes the work among the best of the Rice short pieces and included it in his anthology of the year's best from his magazine. Rice includes so many of the familiar motifs here, and references abound to other Malone cases. Miss Adams, the psychiatrist's secretary with an amazing memory, remembers Malone from *The Big Midget Murders* case, and the crazy character names include Dr. Martin Martin.

Many of the short shorts and several of the short stories have a psychiatrist in them, although the doctor changes with each story. Rice's interest in the field dates from her time at Camarillo and her therapy for alcoholism. Over the years, she saw many more counselors. Her daughter, Nancy Atwill, would graduate years later with a degree in psychology and work as a counselor.

The facility proved good for Rice's mental health in addition to her writing. As she began to improve, Rice didn't just let her good feelings go to waste. She began to get more involved with the people at Rancho, and started working on the fundraising aspects of the facility. Rice had always been a master publicist and she tapped many of her famous mystery friends to help with donations or free press.

In a letter to Ned Guymon, she wrote, "very few people know much of anything about MS - and nobody knows what to do about it. Research clinics are working on it here and in Europe, supported largely by MS Society funds. . . . There are roughly 300,000 reported and diagnosed cases of MS . . . None of those people face any real improvement in the future. The vast majority will get steadily, irrevocably, terribly worse."[4]

In her manic fashion, Rice got involved in the operations of the hospital. Using her writing skills as she began to type again, Rice edited the newsletter at Rancho, which informed the patients of hospital events. She also spent hours trying to help the other patients, through encouragement and letters.

The facility also improved Rice's health by providing her with well-balanced meals three times a day. By the time she arrived at Rancho Los Amigos, Rice suffered from severe malnutrition. Except for the periods where she was in the hospital or cared for by a landlady, she had let alcohol be her meal and frequently skipped cooking and eating. This behavior left her with severe vitamin deficiencies that worsened her bone and nerve conditions. The hospital corrected these problems with proper diet.

For many years Rice had only completed short stories, because of her inability to concentrate on any subject for a length of time and her need for fast cash to pay her bills. With her $150,000 lawsuit pending, Rice no longer worried about money, and she had hours of free time to kill between therapy sessions. Many of the plot ideas from before the time of her marriage to Hank DeMott resurfaced and began to interest her again.

While she stayed at this facility, Rice started plotting a full-length book. Finally, she took her own advice and typed 'Chapter 1' at the top of a page and began writing. Many people in New York, including Lee Wright at Simon & Schuster and her agent at the Scott Meredith agency, hesitated to invest any money in a new Craig Rice book. So many times in the past, a book had remained only a pipe dream lost in alcohol, or existed only to get some ready cash. Both parties had made several advances to the author, without a resulting book or repayment. She still owed some four finished novels that had been due for nearly a decade.

In effect, Rice had to start over in publishing less than a decade after her *Time* cover. Seven years stretched out since her last book, and she had gained a reputation for being unreliable. In order to be taken seriously, Rice needed to finish a novel to sell it, and Rancho Los Amigos provided her with a place to write in relative seclusion. She finished a 20,000-word novella that she showed to New York as a measure of good faith, and they saw a return to the old form. They encouraged her to expand the idea into a full-length book.

"The book goes very well. Lee wrote me one of her long letters - beginning with words like "delectable, delightful, etc.etc." and with as usual a lot of damned good ideas for the revisions. I wrote out a very detailed outline of changes, additions, etc - now I'm waiting to hear what she thinks, and then will dive into the work - which should not take too long."[5]

The novella, *No Motive For Murder*, was the precursor of *Knocked For a Loop*, which appeared two years later. Almost the entire plot remains intact in the shorter form, with the exception of the Justuses and the romantic subplot with Jane Estapoole. Rice rarely included Jake and Helene in her short works, and had added their exploits to novels in the past as an afterthought. For the portion of the book already written, Rice would only modify a word or two in places.

Rice wrote other novellas as well. *Shot in the Dark* shows Rice back in top form. Malone and his blonde for the evening, Dolly Dove, stumble onto a murder while parked to admire a scenic view. Alvin Orvell bursts from the bushes to announce that someone has killed his fiancée, Olive Castleberry, and made off with a fortune in diamonds. Malone and Dolly (who could be a relation of Helene's) decide to investigate, and locate the satchel of diamonds only to discover they are paste replicas and not real gems. Von Flanagan arrives to investigate, and takes the whole crowd in for questioning.

Rice proved again that she was the best at her craft of comedic mystery. Malone wants to return to an evening with Dolly and hurries to solve the case. The one-liners fly as Malone tries to salvage his date. "'Olive!' the stranger [Alvin] said. 'Olive' He lapsed back into his white-faced silence.

"'He probably wants a martini,' Malone growled."[6]

Rice brought back Chicago's finest at their finest and funniest. Von Flanagan constantly complains about his life as a cop. "[Malone] half closed his eyes, and dozed. A few phrases came to him through beautiful dreams of Dolly Dove.

"—If the alderman hadn't owed my old man money —

"—Never asked for a promotion. Especially not to Homicide — . . .

"—Murderers seem to go out of their way to make life hard for me —

"—And they say there's a fortune to be made in chinchilla. You just buy two of them —"[7]

Von Flanagan has some new officers assigned to him, including one that seems to be on the prowl for Miss Dove, but Malone ends the case with his date still intact and enough time to catch the sunrise at Starved Rock. Unfortunately, the happy ending doesn't carry over — Dolly Dove isn't heard from again.

The lawsuit Rice had instituted over her fall at the arena stretched out in court. She made repeated trips to New York for pre-trial examinations and the actual trial. Rice, in her ever-optimistic spirit, placed too much faith on the fact that she would receive the full $150,000 judgment. Given the whimsies of the jury system, only a fraction of that amount could be reasonably expected, especially given her own culpability in the accident. However, reasonability was not in Rice's nature. The can't-be-beat attitude imbued in her characters still ran strong in the author.

Stuart Palmer didn't have the same attitude about her chances for big money. "She lives for her New York lawsuit, with high hopes of getting it made-I don't know if was [sic] the accident where she fell down an elevator shaft into the basement of St. Nicholas' Arena and then was bitten on the situpon by the watchman's dog, or not. Something along those lines. She wants to borrow the money so that her daughter Iris can fly back to testify; what Iris could know about it all is beyond me and so is the quick fifty."[8]

Nancy Atwill moved to Japan in 1954 with her family. Joe Atwill had been given an assignment in Tokyo to set up an office for the family chemical company. With Nancy Atwill gone, Rice put a large effort into getting to know Carolyn, her new daughter-in-law and her family, the Baxters. Rice wrote frequently to Carolyn's parents, telling them how much she enjoyed having David Ferguson Ferguson's wife in the family and how she considered her another daughter. "I always prayed that he would marry just the right girl — and just the right family — for I hold the perhaps old-fashioned feeling that a successful and happy marriage is not just a matter of joining two people — but two families."[9] Rice neglected to mention her own checkered history in the letters. She plays the part of a suffering invalid who wants only the best for her son. The letters have the tone of an ever-protective matriarch of her only son, and the in-laws never heard about Rice's recurring forays into matrimony.

The institution proved helpful to the author in other ways as well. Rice's faith deepened as she stayed at the facility in Hondo. The woman who had doubted the existence of God as a Communist frequently wrote about prayer and praying, and spoke of her faith in God to some of her friends. Rice continued to be fascinated by the Catholic faith and occasionally referred to herself as a Catholic.

However, Rice's faith had not healed her own pains of childhood separation. Rice's mother, Mary Randolph, passed away in June 1955. She had moved back to Rio Vista Ranch, the Arizona ranch she had bought with her husband, Sacha, and had lived there since the late 1940s. Rice's brother, Christopher, and his family lived with Mary Randolph. Half-brother Alex Randolph visited frequently, but never Rice. At the time of Mary Randolph's death, the ranch consisted only of a few acres. She had sold much of the land over the years to cover expenses. She willed the ranch and the remaining land to her two sons, leaving Rice nothing. It was an eternal reminder of her scorn for her only daughter.

In the letters written by her at around that time, Rice never mentioned her birth mother or seemed aware of her mother's death. They hadn't spoken since the *Time* interviews back in 1945. Mary Randolph hadn't bothered to attend Nan Rice's funeral, not acknowledging her debt to the woman who had raised her daughter. Unlike Bosco Craig, she hadn't spent her last days wishing to have fulfilled her dreams. Despite the fact that Mary Randolph's behavior had influenced Rice's life and writings to such a great degree, Rice didn't care about her mother's life or death in any noticeable way.

CHAPTER T W E L V E

"It is a fine thing to be successful, . . ."

Rice continued to live at Rancho Los Amigos as she completed her therapy for nerve damage in 1956. During the course of treatment, she improved to a point and could attend the Southern California chapter of MWA occasionally, accompanied by her daughter Iris. Far from the happy and carefree host of the 1940s, she had become an elder stateswoman of the genre, a white-haired woman, mostly confined to a wheelchair. The boozy battles and the lascivious propositions were a part of the past.

In typical fashion, Rice started working on multiple projects at once. Involved in the local MS chapter, she contacted many of the old writing friends that she hadn't seen since before Camarillo, including Ned Guymon. Her appetite whetted for the mystery, she began to write more. While living at Rancho, Rice completed a Malone novel, *My Kingdom for a Hearse*, and partially finished another, *Knocked for a Loop*.

In his replies, Guymon kept his distance to Rice and refused her requests for monetary assistance in her MS-related projects, expressing his desire to contribute to his own charities. No wonder, Rice still owed him money in 1956 from all his loans in the late 1940s. She had become one of the Guymon charities. Without an income, she hadn't bothered to pay off the debts to her friends.

However, Rice could have paid him off if she had wanted. In 1956, she settled the court case with the owners of the St. Nicholas sports arena regarding her fall onto the concrete. Although she had originally sued for $150,000, the verdict only rendered a fraction of that total, $37,500.

Her writing income improved as well when *Detective Files* devoted an entire issue to her true crime cases. All of the cases had appeared in other magazines in the early 1950s. Judging from the dates of the articles, Rice most likely wrote these herself. The marriage to Lipton had disintegrated long before this point, and it's inconceivable that he would have helped his ex-wife to earn more money under her name. Lipton demanded either notoriety or cash from his dealings with Rice.

The true crime cases in *Detective Files* have the same chatty feel to them as the other crime cases collected in *45 Murderers*. The cases ranged from notorious murderer John Reginald Christie to lesser-known cases like Senga Whittingham, who killed her fellow doctor and lover. Again Rice used her connections in the mystery field, which were fewer than in her peak years, to make the cases come alive with quotes from the police and examiners.

Rice continued to write short stories as well as novels. One short story published during this time was "He Never Went Home." Malone returns in top form, taking care of an innocent client, Susie Snyder, and challenging von Flanagan, who reappears in this story. The police accuse Snyder of killing Dale McDowell, a blackmailing newspaper columnist and radio commentator. The frame-up is almost perfect, with the murder taking place in Susie's apartment and her bread knife as the weapon. Malone uses his connections to spirit the client away and begins to try to solve the case.

"He Never Went Home" has many of the more successful elements of Rice's longer works. The interplay in the story between von Flanagan and Malone makes the reader smile, with Malone alternately trying to get away from and stay right beside von Flanagan during his investigation. The gangster influence that Rice used in so many of the novels appears here also, with the less gritty, more amusing tone that readers expected. In all, "He Never Went Home" showed the public that no one wrote John J. Malone stories like Craig Rice.

Rice wrote another novella in 1956, *The Frightened Millionaire*, which introduced the entire O'Leary clan. When Maggie's family finds a corpse in the bedroom of Maggie's brother, the secretary calls Malone to deal with the situation. The death ties in with their civil suit. Malone represents a client against a millionaire, who had smashed into the car of Malone's client while driving drunk. Malone solves both the murder and his own case with Maggie's help.

Rice includes several of her trademarks in portraying the O'Leary family, depicting no parents for Maggie. Malone's right-hand gal lives with her Aunt Aggie, her grandfather, and her brothers and sisters. Unlike many of the orphaned characters Rice used, Maggie seems at ease with the situation. She doesn't show any resentment for her circumstances. Rice's fascination with religion showed through again, with the O'Leary brothers named Matthew, Mark, Luke, John, and Ron, harking back to the names of the Halvorsen boys in *The Thursday Turkey Murders*. Ron fortunately escaped the name of Acts, although the corpse was discovered in his room, making him the prime suspect.

1957 dawned with the publication of the first Rice novel in almost a decade. *Innocent Bystander* had been released in 1949, written prior to the break-up of the DeMott marriage. Simon & Schuster threw a gala cocktail party to promote the new book. Rice basked in the limelight that had not been hers for so long, inviting all of the mystery writers and friends she had met over her eighteen years in mystery.

My Kingdom for a Hearse deals with Jake's adventures as a television producer, the same career Rice's daughter, Iris, held during the 1950s. Justus wants to put Delora Deanne, spokesmodel for the cosmetics firm of the same name, on the air. When he goes to meet Hazel Swackhammer, the owner of the Delora Deanne cosmetics, he learns that five Delora Deannes make up the model. Each of the girls poses for a body part of the fictitious Miss Deanne. "Rita Jardee, a red-haired, haggard and skinny woman who seemed to be hurrying towards middle age, said, 'Delighted, Mr. Malone,' in the mellow voice that held him and untold thousands spellbound every Saturday night."[1]

While Jake tries to figure out a way to combine the women into one for his TV show, someone starts sending the pieces of Delora

Deanne to Hazel, starting with the model's hands.

My Kingdom For A Hearse has one of Rice's better plots. The pieces of the story fit together as tightly as the parts of Delora Deanne, and not only does Malone find the murderer in the end, but Jake has his television show with a Delora Deanne, and Hazel sponsoring. Iris's background in the television world shows through, with the never-ending list of characters that have a talent and want to be in show business. Starting with von Flanagan, who wants to host a talk show, virtually every one of the series characters has a relative or friend who should be on TV. "Mr. Jake Justus is a big shot. Everybody wants to meet Mr. Justus. Everybody has a relative who wants to meet Mr. Justus. Mr. Justus has a lovely office in the Wrigley Building with his name on the door. In gold letters yet. Mr. Justus has a telephone answering service that says Mr. Justus will call you back, only Mr. Justus never does." [2] Maggie has a brother with a new type of camera, and Joe the Angel proffers his niece as an actress and singer.

Perhaps the one distracting item about the book extends from the plot — the number of characters to keep track of. With five Delora Deannes running around, it gets confusing to try to keep straight which girl has what body part, and where the character is supposed to be. However, watching Rice juggle too many balls at once with style, skill, and a laugh is all part of the fun of a Malone-Jake-Helene book.

One character that does get fleshed out more in this novel is Maggie O'Leary, Malone's long-suffering secretary. Introduced back in *The Wrong Murder*, Maggie received one last name in a short story and another one in the novella, *The Frightened Millionaire*. While she has made a steady progression in the short stories, Maggie blooms in the longer format.

What a last name Rice bequeaths to her!

Rice played another one of her inside jokes in naming Maggie. Throughout the 1940s while Rice turned out books and screenplays at a lightening pace, she employed a secretary by the name of Peggy O'Leary. Rice had a laugh in naming Malone's secretary the same thing. We also learn that Maggie's brother, Luke, has perfected a camera that Jake should investigate as a television producer.

As Rice began to write again, she decided to move out of Rancho and into her son David Ferguson's house. His new family now included

Carolyn and children. By this point, Rice's desire to be published again burned brighter than the Chicago fire. She stopped promoting the MS program and dedicated herself to her books.

Upon her release from Rancho, Rice arranged for Dorothy Hughes to meet her at a local Roman Catholic Church not far from Hondo, California. There she received the Church in a small informal service. "Craig ... had learned she was never confirmed and she wanted to be. She asked me if I'd come down and be her sponsor. So I took the bus down from W.L.A (West Los Angeles) to the town, met her at the church as scheduled, and there, in a large, beautiful, empty church, I followed her down the aisle and said the correct responses and Craig was confirmed."[3] The confirmation culminated from her life at the MS center where Rice had become more religious, seeking answers from God about her condition and her life.

Despite her conversion to Catholicism, the author started drinking almost immediately upon leaving the facility. She went back to her old ways. Booze, writing and men. David Ferguson found her impossible to deal with in addition to the demands of his schooling and job. She soon became too much for the young family. Rice moved in with Iris, who lived alone.

Rice didn't spend a lot of time with Nancy Atwill. Her oldest daughter moved back to Los Angeles from Japan in early 1957. Pregnant with her sixth child, she didn't have much opportunity to see Rice between relocating and taking care of her brood.

Shortly after this, Rice became involved with another man, the last one in her life. A patient from the sanitarium, Rice met him while recuperating at Rancho, although there is no indication of what disease he suffered from. The children tried to avoid the couple because they drank excessively and because they found his theories on UFOs and extraterrestrials disconcerting. On the night of August 28th, 1957, he called Ferguson, asking him to come over to the rental Tudor home he and Rice shared on Serrano Avenue. When Ferguson arrived, he found Rice lying at the bottom of a flight of stairs. According to the Los Angeles Times,

"The mystery writer died amid an odd assortment of memorabilia from her busy life.

A half-dozen books formed a shaky pile on a night stand beside her bed along with a crumpled cigarette package and bottles of pills.

Cigarette butts and kitchen matches were scattered about the room and an empty half-pint vodka bottle stood on her strewn desk with a row of books, including her own "Lucky Stiff," an imitation white rabbit and a miniature Madonna and Child.

Tucked under an ash tray were two yellow checks - one for $60, the other for $410 - signed "Craig Rice" and bearing the notation, 'Returned for nonsufficient funds.'

A brightly colored globe of the world had tumbled to the floor.

Near the fallen world on the blue rug lay a small book, dropped open to the floor, identified by its lively jacket as 'A Family Treasury of Children's Stories.'

On the newly papered pale-blue wall above a false mantel hung a somber oil portrait of a lovely woman of another era [Bosco Craig's painting of Mary]."[4]

An ambulance arrived quickly and Rice was taken to a hospital, where she died in a matter of hours without regaining consciousness. *Newsweek* referred to her death as being of natural causes, but that conclusion is unlikely given the circumstances. A more probable explanation was that it was an accident exacerbated by her alcoholism and inability to walk without falling. Rice had been in a wheelchair until recently and still toddled, unsteady on her feet. Combined with alcohol, her unsteadiness might easily have caused her to trip and fall down the flight of stairs. Indeed, the author confided to her landlord that she had fallen the day before the fatal accident.

Even in death, Rice confounded people who tried to understand her life. The confusion surrounding Rice's death has been made worse by comments from her friends. In his preface to the book of collected Withers-Malone stories, Stuart Palmer refers to Rice's last illness. While this might have been a euphemism for death, Rice's accident could hardly be called an illness.

The coroner performed an autopsy on Rice after finding bloodstains on the carpet and on Rice's purse. The death certificate lists a series of life-threatening conditions that Rice suffered from at the time of her death. Rice's kidneys had been damaged from the years of alcohol abuse and among the diseases she had contracted were pyelonephritis and pulmonary edema, both ailments that stem from renal disease. Given the serious nature of these ailments, she probably didn't have long to live.

The specter of suicide loomed over her death as well. Rice had attempted suicide twice after her break-up with DeMott, and at least twice more while living in New York after her nosedive onto the cement floor. In addition, sufferers of bipolar disorder have a significantly higher rate of suicide than the general population. Her death at the young age of forty-nine only fueled speculations.

On the same night as Rice's death, Jack Follows arrived in Los Angeles, tracked down by his daughters. They had communicated briefly, and he decided to fly out to meet Nancy and Iris as well as to have a reunion with his ex-wife. When he arrived at the airport, Nancy Atwill took him to her home. As the television played in the background, father and daughter were astounded to hear that mystery writer Craig Rice had been found dead in her home. Nancy Atwill would later relate how Follows's face showed the obvious love he still felt for his former wife. That someone could love a woman after a twenty-five year separation following a disastrous marriage, and still hope for a reconciliation was a fitting epitaph to this author. Both captivating and infuriating, Craig Rice defied description, yet friends remembered her generosity of spirit and her sad untimely end.

Rice was buried with a small family ceremony, in a plot with no marker. Iris's husband, Howard Metcalfe, would install a monument on Rice's tomb many years later, shortly after Iris's death at age 62 from cancer.

Two weeks after Rice's death, the second Malone book of 1957 came out, *Knocked for a Loop*. Rice had expanded her earlier "No Motive For Murder." The book deals with Leonard Estapoole, a self-righteous man who has been gathering information on the Chicago underworld in his quest to shut the ganglands down. The underworld appears to be fighting back when Alberta Cammanday, Leonard's stepchild, disappears from home, and the ransom note demands Leonard's information on the mob. The kidnapers choose Malone as the go-between for the kidnapping, since he has been a target of Leonard Estapoole's investigation and animosity exists between the two men.

When Malone shows up at his office, the room looks like the scene of a fight, with Estapoole dead on the floor. Malone tidies it up, and after a night's adventures, returns to discover the office as he originally discovered it the night before. He reluctantly gets help from Max Hook, in the form of a twenty-four hour signed confession from one of Hook's associates. Without the worry of interference from the police, Malone then goes about trying to solve the case.

The book uses a highly original plot device that twists the idea Rice used in *Having Wonderful Crime*, *The Lucky Stiff*, and several of the short stories. Rice's years of mystery criticism had given her a better appreciation for plot twists and how to execute them.

The book lacked the varied backgrounds that had become a tradition in her books. So many of Rice's novels contained settings that reflected her life at the time, yet most of this book's backdrop consists of the Loop and the Estapoole mansion, harkening back to her first book, *8 Faces*, and the Inglehart mansion.

Despite the bland backdrop, the book shines as one of Rice's better efforts. The plot and characters mesh well, and the reader gets a feel for the characters in some depth. Rice blended the more realistic elements of the plot with her far-fetched humorous points better than she had in *The Lucky Stiff*. Malone's romance remains a dalliance and a search for a proper tearoom to impress the object of his affection. "Jane would be Junior League. That fitted. It made one more thing he approved of about her, along with the shining, well-brushed hair, the flawless make-up, the perfectly selected clothes, and the gentle voice. He'd never met a girl exactly like her before, never had a chance to really get acquainted with one. A thoroughly nice girl, that was it. He half-shut his eyes for a moment, and did a little dreaming about Jane Estapoole"[5]

Rice's dealings with the underworld characters in her books often received criticism for being unrealistic or highly imaginative. The reasons behind the charge become apparent here. Max Hook, that mountain of a man, decorates his penthouse in Early Colonial in this novel. However, comparing Rice's hardboiled to that of a Hammett or Chandler is like comparing Abbott and Costello's Dracula to the original novel. While both vehicles have the same source, one seeks to amuse while the other has a serious purpose of enlightenment. To have actual underworld figures in one of the Rice novels would have thrown the fictional world out of kilter. Either the other characters would appear very shallow, or the humor would have to be lost to the realism.

Unfortunately, Rice didn't live to see publication and the good reviews, stating that Craig Rice was back in top form. The hard years had culminated with a great comeback, which Rice missed.

CHAPTER THIRTEEN

"Imitations of Fiction"

Few authors have been as prodigious in the afterlife as Craig Rice. Her fans refused to let her go softly into the history of the genre. At the time of her death, as promised to Lee Wright many years before, Rice had partially completed a Bingo-Handsome book.

The book, entitled *The April Robin Murders*, featured Bingo and Handsome in Hollywood, their final destination in their cross-country trip, which had begun fifteen years before. Working as she normally did, Rice wrote the manuscript without the aid of a synopsis or notes of any kind, preferring to keep the ideas and plot twists locked in her head. Unfortunately, she took the solution to this mystery to her grave.

This presented a predicament for editor Lee Wright, who now worked for Random House. Mysteries need endings and she didn't want another *Mystery of Edwin Drood* on her hands. Finding a writer who could imitate Rice's humorous style while being creative enough to solve the case and write a plausible ending to the book proved a formidable challenge.

Lee sought out Evan Hunter (who ironically had been the man who met Rice at the Scott Meredith literary agency). Evan was a hot young writer at that time. *The Blackboard Jungle* had been recently published, along with another novel under the Hunter name. Under the pseudonym of Ed McBain, he had begun the 87th Precinct series in the 1950s and received critical acclaim for those books. Rice's friend, Anthony Boucher, regularly listed the McBain books in his top ten books of the year for most of the 1950s and 1960s. Hunter remembers the offer from Lee Wright. "She [Lee] knew my work, she knew I wouldn't screw it up. It just seemed a challenge. When I was writing for the pulp magazines, you could either become a hack or you could learn something and I decided that I was going to learn something in every pulp story I wrote. I think that this was just another assignment - to see if I could finish this book without knowing who the killer is in the same style as the person who started it."[1]

Hunter says that he cannot remember where he started and Rice left off. Trying to detect a change in style provides a secondary mystery for the reader. He wrote the rest of the novel without changing anything that Rice had written to that point, only adding the last several chapters. From reviewing the style, chapter endings and personal preferences, he estimates that he started around page 126 of the book, but he can't swear to a particular page or chapter.

The book resembles the other books in the series. After arriving in Hollywood, Riggs and Kuzak lose a large sum of money to a phony real-estate agent who "sells" them a mansion once owned by silent screen star, April Robin. As the men try to recover their money and stay on at the house, they realize they have "purchased" the house where Julian Lattimer and his fifth wife, Lois, had lived. Julian had mysteriously disappeared, presumed murdered, and Lois had been investigated for his mysterious end until she fled town with a large sum of money.

The best of the series, the book combines some of the better elements from the other books. The use of old crimes and their ramifications seemed to be an ongoing theme in the books. The Julian Lattimer case occurred a few years prior to Bingo and Handsome's purchase of the house. Everyone is waiting for the seven-year waiting period to be up, much as they were with the Pigeon character in *The Sunday Pigeon*

Murders. A great deal of money disappeared with Lois Lattimer, and no one knows what became of the cash or the widow, similar to the robbery loot in *The Thursday Turkey Murders.* Adelle Lattimer, Julian's fourth ex-wife, is owed thousands by her ex-husband in back alimony if he is alive, and is to receive a portion of his estate if he has died. So she hires the duo to find clues in their house to Julian's whereabouts. Bingo and Handsome will receive a share of the fourth wife's back alimony if they can find Julian.

Rice poked fun at the movie-making industry in this novel, an industry that had long given her fits. Over the course of fifteen years, she had her share of films made and optioned, usually with much ado and always with problems. She poked fun at the way deals were made by involving top Hollywood agent Leo Henkin, who seems to know everything in Hollywood as soon as it happens. "If you're looking for talent, . . . if you're looking for stories, if you're looking for new faces or old faces, Leo Henkin can help you. . . . Leo Henkin knows everybody and everything that goes on, . . ."[2] Bingo talks a great story with agent Leo Henkin, and they spend all their money trying to set themselves up in Hollywood.

When Bingo and Handsome sign a talent who has grown up right under Hollywood's nose, Hunter allows the series to end on a high note. With Bingo and Handsome set for life managing their new property, the reader can be glad for the pair.

Some of Rice's finished short stories existed too. She'd written a great deal in the months at Rancho, and she'd passed the work on to her agent. Some of it was already scheduled for publication before her death, whereas other pieces were sold following the accident. In "Wry Highball," Malone investigates an impossible crime in which arsenic is found in the drink of millionaire Arthur Bent. Both of his girlfriends had been present at the scene of the crime, and Malone refuses to believe either of the beautiful women could have killed the man. Malone locates more motives for the crime and solves the murder with his superior knowledge of alcohol and drink mixing.

"They're Trying to Kill Me" appeared in 1959 in *The Saint Mystery Magazine.* Rodney Melcher, a Lake Forest resident, hires Malone to investigate some murder attempts by one of the members of the Melcher household. When Melcher's brother turns up dead in

Rodney's room, von Flanagan suspects that Rodney consulted Malone in order to better plan his brother's death. Malone investigates and discovers the real killer.

Rice didn't get to see this story in print, although the plot dealt with one of her favorite mystery subjects, the cliché of her chosen genre. By reading so many mysteries, Rice saw a number of elements that seemed to crop up repeatedly in novels. To someone as quick-witted as Rice, this commonality amused her. In "They're Trying to Kill Me," the butler commits the crime. In her days at Rancho, Rice corresponded with Fred Dannay to locate books in which the butler did it for the other residents at the facility. She also expressed an interest in writing a book in which all the clichés of the genre (untraceable poisons, sinister servants, mysterious Asians, etc.) could be packed into a single novel, an achievement she never fulfilled.

The flip side of the cliché, "The Butler Who Didn't Do It," appeared the next year. While the motivations in the story don't hold up, James Dohr, a butler, is murdered shortly after the death of his employer. The police accuse his wife of the crime, but Malone investigates the employer's family since the butler excelled in collecting household secrets.

With her death, some of Rice's books started to disappear from print. One of the problems with the Rice estate continued to be Rice's lack of records. Most authors keep detailed records of their books and sales, but not Rice. The last decade of her life, punctuated by frequent moves, incarcerations, and hospital stays left Rice with virtually no papers or documentation of her contracts and publications. In a letter to Guymon late in her life, she admitted that she hadn't even kept first editions of all of her own work. Therefore, Rice's children found it difficult to properly promote the author without a proper accounting of her novels and short stories. The novels were easier to trace, especially the popular Malone series. Even so, the children had moved on with their own lives and were not anxious to spend countless hours trying to make sense of Rice's literary estate.

A full cross-reference of all of Rice's short stories still cannot be compiled. Even the Scott Meredith Agency did not have a full accounting of her works, because she sometimes sold work on her own to keep all of the profits herself when she needed cash. Work has been done in

regard to a complete listing of short stories to clear up some of the
confusion regarding these stories, but without records, the effort
becomes a matter of hit and miss. Rice sometimes resold stories, making for duplicate listing. At other times, she didn't tell her agent
because she wanted the money.

So new Rice stories may crop up in small digests without prior
notice. It's impossible to scour all of the magazines of the 1940s and
1950s to complete the list. In other cases, Rice was given a publishing
credit where none existed. One short story collection was listed that
was never published in this country, adding to the confusion. This
biography has tried to put together a fairly comprehensive list, but
makes no claims to having a full list. Every effort has been made to find
as many stories as possible, and document them with the actual text of
the story.

Rights and royalties to her other books also presented a problem.
Rice didn't keep copies of her book contracts, including the novels
written for other people. Hence, rumors like the Gypsy Rose Lee novels
can become apocryphal after time. Some of her novels can be found in
libraries and private collections, and others seem to have totally disappeared. According to her letters, she earned half the royalties of the
Sanders book, but didn't keep copies of the contracts to prove the fact
or collect from later editions. Lipton's claims to the estate confuse the
matter further, because the death of both primary parties nullified
those contracts. Contracts like that with Cleve Cartmill and Evan
Hunter only serve to confuse things more.

Enough records and copies of her work existed to put together a
short story collection of Malone works entitled *The Name is Malone*.
The book came out in 1958 as a paperback original from Pyramid
Books. The collection contained ten stories: "The Murder of Mr.
Malone," "The Tears of Evil," "His Heart Could Break," "Good-bye
Forever," "And The Birds Still Sing," "He Never Went Home," "Life Can
Be Horrible," "Good-Bye, Good-Bye," "The Bad Luck Murders" and
"The End of Fear." The collection was made up of short stories that
Rice had published in *Ellery Queen* and *Manhunt*, so the lineage of the
pieces was easy to trace. Additionally since Dannay had purchased the
cream of the Rice stories for *Ellery Queen's Mystery Magazine*, many of
the stories in the collection represent Rice at the top of her form.

As for her other short stories, friend Stuart Palmer continued to write the Withers-Malone stories after Rice's death. He maintained that Rice had supplied ideas for several more short stories before her death, in the form of letters and notes to Palmer. "Rice's real contribution to the stories, apart from the unique character of Malone (and the faithful Maggie), was in the gimmicks, the gadgets, the slant... Oddly enough, it is in the last one we did—"Withers and Malone—Crime-Busters"[1963]— that Rice had most to say about it all."[3]

All six of the Palmer-Rice stories were published as a short story volume in 1963 as *People vs. Withers & Malone.* An introduction written by long-time friend Fred Dannay (in the person of Ellery Queen) contained a slight amount of biographical information on the two writers. A Preface written by Palmer explained how mostly he wrote the stories. Since the stories continued after Rice's death with no appreciable change in style, this fact was an obvious admission.

The last two stories in the collection were the least true to the character of Malone. In one of the two stories written after Rice's death, "Withers and Malone, Brainstormers," Hildegarde finds Malone on her doorstep, on the run from the police and a variety of criminal types. His client and lover, Nancy Jorgens, has skipped bail and Chicago to trace down her former lover and the father of her child, because he has brought forgery charges against her for passing a check with his name on it. Malone and Withers find her, with a gun in her hand, over the dead body of her lover. There are no bullet holes in the corpse.

An unusual story for the pair has Malone appearing in court to plead a case. In the entire Rice canon, no courtroom scenes exist in which Malone practices law. Yet in this story, Palmer has a very limited amount of legal drama. In less than a page of text, the lawyer quickly asks for a recess to solve the murder, but nevertheless, he appears in court. The case also ends with Malone and Nancy planning a wedding. Palmer tried to marry off his characters on more than one occasion, having attempted to marry Withers and Oscar Piper at the end of their first case. However, a married Malone, no matter how beautiful the bride, remains inconceivable.

For these reasons, the story shows itself as the weakest of the half dozen. The spectacular crime in which only one person could have been guilty of the murder turns out to be no crime at all, with no one arrested for the various illegalities. The reader feels cheated by the solution of the crime, although technically it is an interesting solution.

Palmer published the last of the combined stories in 1963, a story originally entitled "Withers and Malone, Crimebusters," later retitled "People vs. Withers and Malone" for the collection. The story opens with Malone on the verge of losing his first client, Junior Coleman.

Tried for the murder of his lover, who was run down by Coleman's car, the accused received a life sentence. Malone contacts the man and offers his services in getting a second trial. At the retrial, the court hands down the penalty to Coleman when a witness testifies that Malone tried to bribe him. With the execution only days away, and the feisty lawyer facing disbarment, Hildegarde Withers rides into town to save the day. When the perjuring witness dies with Malone knocked out cold beside him, Malone goes to the hospital under police watch. The case sets a trap for a murderer, rather than relying on the deductions of the sleuths, but the interplay between the two characters still amuses.

Pastiches of Rice's work appeared as well. *The Pickled Poodles* written in 1960 by Larry Harris, an acquaintance of Rice's, used the Malone and Justus characters in a tribute to Craig Rice. Harris freelanced at the time, having been an agent at the Scott Meredith Agency, where he had met Rice. He recounts that he had an idea for a novel and Malone continued to push his way into the book. Lee Wright showed skepticism of the idea at first, but Harris won her over.

The children gave permission to use the characters after reading advance copies of the book and the novel was published at Random House under the editorial eye of Lee Wright, who had changed houses in the late 1950s. Like many of the originals, the book is currently out of print.

In 1967, one last Malone novel by Rice appeared as a paperback original, *But the Doctor Died*. The book was purportedly found in a trunk, written by Rice in the 1940s, when she wrote most of her novels. However, where that trunk might have been is only speculative. Rice, at the top of her form, did not write this novel. Any belongings she might have had were lost along the trail of destruction she left after her stint at Camarillo. The story of the find is extremely suspect.

Sadly, this last effort doesn't evoke the fun of Malone and the

Justuses from the war years. Anthony Boucher wrote, "One is apt to be suspicious of such finds, especially since the scandal of the "Posthumous" Sherlock Holmes story which proved to be wholly unauthentic..."[4] The plot barely covers one hundred fifty pages, thin even for a Rice story. Spies recruit Helene to keep an eye on her friend, Vivian Conover. The Cold War plot line is ironic, given the FBI's opinion of Rice. Conover finds herself involved with a spy ring led by a man who once stiffed Malone out of his fee. Malone may not have ever lost a client, but obviously he lost more than one client's fee.

The book fails on many levels. The work most resembles an abortive first draft of a Rice novel, one to which the fun still needs to be added. The tone resembles neither the lighthearted devil-may-care attitude of the other books or the gritty style Rice used for some of her hardboiled work. No puns or malapropisms come from the little lawyer or the usually wisecracking Justuses. Von Flanagan doesn't elaborate about his new career plans. Moreover, Helene becomes too submissive and Jake, who has worshiped his wife for eleven novels suddenly seems uninterested in her. While the book could be a passable spy/thriller novel, it definitely isn't Rice material.

Certain elements lead the reader to the conclusion that the novel postdates Rice's last Malone book. First, Ma Blodgett shows up and mentions, "This one's older and prettier. I doubt if you'll leave her here long."[5] Ma Blodgett appeared only once, in *Knocked For a Loop* where she hides Alberta Commanday. *Loop* didn't hit the shelves until after Rice's death in 1957, making it unlikely that Rice wrote *Doctor Died*. In addition, plot devices include computers and microdots, elements that wouldn't have been available in the 1940s when Rice supposedly wrote this book.

Despite the many attempts to keep one of the best loved trios in the mystery world alive, the exploits of Malone and the Justuses could only have been written by the manic genius of Craig Rice. When she left this world, their adventures stopped. As Fred Dannay wrote of her after her death, "Oh, how she is missed these unfunny days; she was a wild, wacky, wonderful woman; she was gay, impulsive, generous, often reckless; she was fearful and courageous; and she was foolish and wise beyond her years."[6]

Unlike the life of Agatha Christie, who Rice rivaled in the mid-

1940s, little has been done to untangle the Rice's life. Perhaps this is because the task seems overwhelming or impossible. Rice left a small legacy beyond her misleading *Time* article and a few letters. Only a few articles about her life have appeared, each more derivative of the *Time* piece than the last. Her life, so innovative and unusual, has remained a mystery like the lady herself.

If Rice had been born later, her life might have been different. So much has been done in the area of manic depression and its treatment that Rice could have led a more normal life. With chemical help, her reputation for drinking and wild behavior might not have overshadowed her career. However, it's difficult to speculate. A more stable Rice might not have had the comedic talents that shine in her books. She might have lost the skill or her wit through medication. A more balanced Rice over a longer career might have written many more books to make us smile. A troubled woman, but one who had great talent, should not be ignored. She paved the way for many women writers in mystery today, with her firm beliefs and her will to succeed. In the genre today, many women support each other and help with promotions and publicity. Rice's special place in mystery, with her *Time* cover and her comedic talent, would have assured her a following in any era.

Footnotes

INTRODUCTION
1 "Mulled Murder, with Spice.", Time, January 28, 1946. pg 86. (All subsequent chapter subheads are taken from the same article with the
   same attribution)

CHAPTER 1
1 "Mulled Murder, with Spice.", Time, January 28, 1946. pg 86.
2 Personal letter from Craig Rice to Fred Dannay, dated Friday the 23rd,
   no year. Dannay collection. Manuscripts department, Columbia
   University, New York City, New York.

CHAPTER 2
1 "Mulled Murder, with Spice.", Time, January 28, 1946. pg 84.
2 "Murder Makes Merry", **The Art of the Mystery Story**, edited by Howard
   Haycraft, pg 241.

CHAPTER 3
1 "Murder Makes Merry", **The Art of the Mystery Story**, edited by Howard
   Haycraft, pg 242.
2 "His Heart Could Break", **The Name is Malone**, (Pyramid Books, New
   York, 1958), page 40.
3 **The Fourth Postman**, (Simon & Schuster, New York, 1948), page 237.
4 **8 Faces at 3**, (Simon & Schuster, New York, 1939), pages 12-13.
5 "It's a Mystery to Me", The Writer, 57, November 1944, page 324-325.
6 **8 Faces At 3**, (Simon & Schuster, New York, 1939), page 14.
7 **8 Faces At 3**, (Simon & Schuster, New York, 1939), page 39.
8 **8 Faces At 3**, (Simon & Schuster, New York, 1939), page 46.
9 **8 Faces At 3**, (Simon & Schuster, New York, 1939), page 69.
10 The Lucky Stiff, (Simon & Schuster, New York, 1945), page 209.
11 Wright, Lee. "Editorial Approval," **Murderess Ink**. Editor: Dilys Winn
   (Workman Publishing Co., New York, 1979), page 72.
12 Personal letter from Lawrence Lipton to Craig Rice, dated February 1st,
   1939. Lipton letters, Special Collections, USC, Los Angeles, California.

CHAPTER 4
1 **The Corpse Steps Out**, (Simon & Schuster, New York, 1940), page 118.
2 **The Corpse Steps Out**, (Simon & Schuster, New York, 1940), page 118.
3 **The Corpse Steps Out**, (Simon & Schuster, New York, 1940), page 29.
4 **The Wrong Murder**, (Simon & Schuster, New York, 1940), page 19.
5 **The Wrong Murder**, (Simon & Schuster, New York, 1940), page 1.
6 **The Wrong Murder**, (Simon & Schuster, New York, 1940), page 244.
7 **The Wrong Murder**, (Simon & Schuster, New York, 1940), page 9.
8 **The Right Murder**, (Simon & Schuster, New York, 1940), page 280.
9 **The Right Murder**, (Simon & Schuster, New York, 1940), page 310.
10 **Trial By Fury**, (Simon & Schuster, New York, 1941) page 108.

11 **Trial By Fury**, (Simon & Schuster, New York, 1941) page 109.

12 **Trial By Fury**, (Simon & Schuster, New York, 1941) page 13.

13 **Trial By Fury**, (Simon & Schuster, New York, 1941), page 268.

14 Personal letter from Lawrence Lipton to Margot Johnson of the Ann Watkins Agency, dated February 21st, 1941. Lipton letters, Special Collections, USC, Los Angeles, California.

15 Lee, Gypsy Rose. "All About Gypsy, Craig Rice, and a Dog Named Bill," <u>New York Post</u>, November 19th, 1941.

16 Auden, W.H. "The Guilty Vicarage", **The Dyer's Hand**, (Vintage Books, New York, 1989) p. 146.

17 Promotional materials sent from Simon & Schuster to reviewers, a letter dated February 19th, 1941.

18 **The G-String Murders**, (Simon & Schuster, New York, 1941), page 7.

19 **Gypsy: A Memoir**, page 252.

20 Review written by Jack Ketch, no date or paper known.

CHAPTER 5

1 **The Big Midget Murders**, (Simon & Schuster, New York, 1942), page 297-298..

2 **The Big Midget Murders**, (Simon & Schuster, New York, 1942), page 191.

3 Personal letter from Craig Rice to Margot Johnson, dated January 19th, 1944. Watkins collection. Manuscripts department, Columbia University, New York City, New York.

4 **The Sunday Pigeon Murders**, (Simon & Schuster, New York, 1942), page 60.

5 **The Sunday Pigeon Murders**, (Simon & Schuster, New York, 1942), page 61.

6 **To Catch a Thief**, (Dial Press, New York, 1942), page 31.

7 **To Catch a Thief**, (Dial Press, New York, 1942), page 288.

8 **The Man Who Slept All Day**, (Coward McCann, New York, 1942), page 147.

9 Personal letter from Craig Rice to Fred Dannay, dated Tuesday the 13th, no year. Dannay collection. Manuscripts department, Columbia University, New York City, New York.

10 **Murder Through the Looking Glass**, (Coward McCann, New York, 1943), page 87.

11 **Murder Through the Looking Glass**, (Coward McCann, New York, 1943), page 109.

12 Rodell, Marie. **Mystery Fiction: Theory and Technique**, (Hermiatage House, New York, 1952), page 91.

13 **Having Wonderful Crime**, (Simon & Schuster, New York, 1943), page 270.

14 Promotional materials sent from Simon & Schuster to reviewers, a letter dated February 19th, 1941.

15 **Telefair**, (Bobbs-Merrill, Indianapolis, 1942), page 76.

16 "Mulled Murder, With Spice", <u>Time</u>. January 28th, 1946. page 84.

17 **Mother Finds A Body**, (Simon & Schuster, New York, 1943), page 21.

18 **The Thursday Turkey Murders**, (Simon & Schuster, New York,

1943), page 168.
19 **The Thursday Turkey Murders**, (Simon & Schuster, New York, 1943), page 301.
20 "His Heart Could Break", **The Name is Malone**, (Pyramid Books, New York, 1958), page 37.

CHAPTER 6
1 "It's a Mystery to Me", by Craig Rice. <u>Chicago Daily News</u>, July 7, 1943.
2 "It's a Mystery to Me", by Craig Rice. <u>Chicago Daily News</u>, May 10, 1944.
3 "It's a Mystery to Me", by Craig Rice. <u>Chicago Daily News</u>, November 3, 1943.
4 Personal letter from Dorothy Hughes to the author, dated January 7th, 1993.
5 Quote from Francis Tower Laney,
6 Personal letter from A.P. White to Craig Rice, dated October 21st, 1944. White mss. Manuscripts department, Lilly Library, Indiana University, Bloomington, Indiana.
7 **Home Sweet Homicide**, (Simon & Schuster, New York, 1944), page 298.
8 "Mulled Murder, With Spice", Time Magazine. January 28th, 1946. page 85.
9 **Home Sweet Homicide**, (Simon & Schuster, New York, 1944), page 1.
10 **Home Sweet Homicide**, (Simon & Schuster, New York, 1944), page 212.
11 Letter from Craig Rice to Margot Johnson of the Ann Watkins Agency dated March 31st, 1944. Watkins collection, Manuscripts department, Columbia University, New York City, NY.
12 "It's a Mystery to Me", <u>The Writer</u>, 57, November 1944, page 324-325.
13 "It's a Mystery to Me", <u>The Writer</u>, 57, November 1944, page 324-325.
14 Personal letter from Craig Rice to Ned Guymon, dated February 4th, 1945. Guymon collection, Popular Press Library, Bowling Green State University, Bowling Green, Ohio.
15 Personal letter from Craig Rice to Ned Guymon, dated August 3rd, 1945. Guymon collection, Popular Press Library, Bowling Green State University, Bowling Green, Ohio.
16 **The Lucky Stiff**, (Simon & Schuster, New York, 1945), page 29-30.
17 **The Lucky Stiff**, (Simon & Schuster, New York, 1945), page 32-33.
18 Personal letter from Craig Rice to Ned Guymon, dated February 5th, 1945. Guymon collection, Popular Press Library, Bowling Green State University, Bowling Green, Ohio.
19 **Crime on My Hands**, (Simon & Schuster, New York, 1944), page 60.
20 "It's a Mystery to Me", by Craig Rice. Chicago Daily News, October 11, 1944.
21 **Jethro Hammer**, (Coward McCann, New York, 1944), page 72.
22 **Jethro Hammer**, (Coward McCann, New York, 1944), page 238.
23 **Jethro Hammer**, (Coward McCann, New York, 1944), page 238.

CHAPTER 7
1 Reporter notes for <u>Time</u> cover story, from Jim Felton to William Chapman, Time morgue, dated March 32, 1945.

2 "Mulled Murder, with Spice.", Time, January 28, 1946. pg 84.
3 "Mulled Murder, with Spice.", Time, January 28, 1946. pg 84.
4 "Mulled Murder, with Spice.", Time, January 28, 1946. pg 86.
5 "Mulled Murder, with Spice.", Time, January 28, 1946. pg 84.
6 Time, February 10, 1947, people section.
7 Radio Life, February 29, 1948, page 11.
8 "City Split on Heirens Guilt", The Chicago American, July 19, 1946.
9 Hughes, **Dorothy B., Erle Stanley Gardner: The Case of the Real Perry Mason**, (William Morrow, New York, 1978), page 210.
10 "Wuxtry! Read All About It!", Time, July 29, 1946. pg 61.
11 "Wuxtry! Read All About It!", Time, July 29, 1946. pg 61.
12 Los Angeles Murders, (Duell, Sloan, and Pierce, New York, 1947), page 5.

CHAPTER 8

1 Guymon, E.T. Jr. "The Lucky Stiff," **Murderess Ink**. Editor: Dilys Winn (Workman Publishing, New York, 1979), page 73.
2 Personal letter from Craig Rice to Ned Guymon, dated July 12, 1949. Guymon collection, Popular Press Library, Bowling Green State University, Bowling Green, Ohio
3 Personal letter from Craig Rice to Fred Dannay, dated Friday the 23rd, no year. Dannay collection. Manuscripts department, Columbia University, New York City, New York.
4 Personal letter from Craig Rice to Ned Guymon, dated November 26th, 1948. Guymon collection, Popular Press Library, Bowling Green State University, Bowling Green, Ohio
5 Personal letter from Ned Guymon to Craig Rice, dated November 23rd, 1948. Guymon collection, Popular Press Library, Bowling Green State University, Bowling Green, Ohio.
6 Personal letter from Ned Guymon to Craig Rice, dated November 26th, 1948. Guymon collection, Popular Press Library, Bowling Green State University, Bowling Green, Ohio.
7 **The Fourth Postman**, (Simon & Schuster, New York, 1948), page 135.
8 **The Fourth Postman**, (Simon & Schuster, New York, 1948), page 112.
9 Personal letter from Craig Rice to Lee Wright of Simon & Schuster, dated February 19th, Lipton letters, Special Collections, USC, Los Angeles, California.
10 **Innocent Bystander**, (Simon & Schuster, New York, 1949), page 10.
11 **Innocent Bystander**, (Simon & Schuster, New York, 1949), page 47.
12 Preface, People vs. Withers and Malone, (Simon & Schuster, New York, 1963), page 14.
13 "Once Upon a Train", **People vs. Withers and Malone**, (Simon & Schuster, New York, 1963), page 23.
14 "Good-bye, Good-bye!", **The Name is Malone**, (Pyramid Books, New York, 1958), page 137.

CHAPTER 9

1 Personal letter from Craig Rice to Ned Guymon, dated May 22nd, 1950. Guymon collection, Popular Press Library, Bowling Green State University, Bowling Green, Ohio.
2 Personal letter from Stuart Palmer to Ned Guymon, dated June 15th,

1951. Guymon collection, Popular Press Library, Bowling Green State University, Bowling Green, Ohio.
3 Personal letter from Lawrence Lipton to Craig Rice, dated 12/10/51, Lipton letters, Special Collections, USC, Los Angeles, California.
4 Personal letter from Stuart Palmer to Ned Guymon. Guymon collection, Popular Press Library, Bowling Green State University, Bowling Green, Ohio
5 "Cherchez La Frame", **People vs. Withers and Malone**, (Simon & Schuster, New York, 1963), page 23.

CHAPTER 10
1 Personal letter from Craig Rice to Ned Guymon, dated November 20th, 1953. Guymon collection, Popular Press Library, Bowling Green State University, Bowling Green, Ohio
2 "Girl Loses Boy", **45 Murderers**, (Simon & Schuster, New York, 1952), page 282.
3 "The Black Dahlia Case", **45 Murderers**, (Simon & Schuster, New York, 1952), page 282.
4 Personal letter from Lawrence Lipton to Craig Rice, dated 12/10/51. Lipton letters, Special Collections, USC, Los Angeles, California.
5 Personal conversation between the author and Evan Hunter, conducted October 9th, 1993 in Omaha, NE at Bouchercon 24.
6 Cooper, John and Pike, B.A., **Detective Fiction:The Collector's Guide**, (Barn Owl Books, Somerset, England, 1988), p. 158.
7 "The Bells Are Ringing", <u>Manhunt</u>, November, 1953. pg 42.
8 "The Dead Undertaker", <u>The Saint</u>, April-May, 1967. pg 77.
9 Personal letter from Stuart Palmer to A.P. White from November 19, 1953. White collection, Lilly Library, Indiana University, Bloomington, Indiana.
10 Personal letter from Stuart Palmer to Ned Guymon from June, 1953. Guymon collection, Popular Press Library, Bowling Green State University, Bowling Green, Ohio

CHAPTER 11
1 Personal letter from Craig Rice to Fred Dannay, dated July 11, 1955. Dannay collection. Manuscripts department, Columbia University, New York City, New York.
2 Personal letter from Stuart Palmer to Ned Guymon, dated July 5th, 1955. Guymon collection, Popular Press Library, Bowling Green State University, Bowling Green, Ohio
3 "The Last Man Alive", **My Best Murder Story**, page 306.
4 Personal letter from Craig Rice to Ned Guymon, dated July 5th, 1956. Guymon collection, Popular Press Library, Bowling Green State University, Bowling Green, Ohio
5 Personal letter from Craig Rice to Lawrence Lipton, dated Wednesday. Lipton letters, Special Collections, USC, Los Angeles, California.
6 "Shot in the Dark", <u>Manhunt</u>, August, 1955. pg 60.
7 "Shot in the Dark", <u>Manhunt</u>, August, 1955. pg 71.
8 Personal letter from Stuart Palmer to Ned Guymon, dated November, 1955. Guymon collection, Popular Press Library, Bowling Green State University, Bowling Green, Ohio

9 Personal letter from Craig Rice to Margaret Baxter, dated June 19th, 1955. Personal collection of David Ferguson / Lauren Alexandra, California.

CHAPTER 12
1 **My Kingdom for a Hearse**, (Simon & Schuster, New York, 1957), page 7.
2 **My Kingdom for a Hearse**, (Simon & Schuster, New York, 1957), page 23.
3 Personal letter from Dorothy B. Hughes to the author dated January 7th, 1993.
4 "Mystery Writer's Death Mystery - for Awhile", **Los Angeles Times**, August 30th, 1957, page 1.
5 **Knocked for a Loop**, (Simon & Schuster, New York, 1957), page 133.

CHAPTER 13
1 Personal conversation between the author and Evan Hunter, conducted October 9th, 1993 in Omaha, NE at Bouchercon 24.
2 **The April Robin Murders**, (Random House, New York, 1958), page 75.
3 Introduction, **People vs. Withers & Malone**, (Simon & Schuster, New York, 1963), page 14-15.
4 "Criminals At Large", Anthony Boucher review column, dated March 26th, 1967. New York Times.
5 **But the Doctor Died**, (Lancet, New York, 1967), page 117.
6 Introduction, **People vs. Withers & Malone**, (Simon & Schuster, New York, 1963), page 8.

Craig Rice Novels

8 Faces at 3
(Death at Three; also Murder Stops the Clock) . .1939
The Corpse Steps Out 1940
The Wrong Murder 1940
The Right Murder 1941
Trial By Fury 1941
    (Haycraft-Queen Cornerstone Library Selection)
The Big Midget Murders 1942
The Sunday Pigeon Murders 1942
Telefair (Yesterday's Murder) 1942
The Man Who Slept All Day 1942
    (As Michael Venning)
Having Wonderful Crime 1943
To Catch a Thief 1943
    (As Daphne Sanders)
The Thursday Turkey Murders 1943
Murder Through the Looking Glass 1943
    (As Michael Venning)
Jethro Hammer 1944
    (As Michael Venning)
Home Sweet Homicide 1944
    (Haycraft-Queen Cornerstone Library Selection)
Crime on My Hands 1944
    (ghosted for George Saunders)
The Lucky Stiff 1945
Los Angeles Murders 1947
    (editor of true crime collection)
The Fourth Postman 1948
Innocent Bystander 1949
45 Murderers 1952
    (a collection of true crime stories)
Knocked for a Loop (The Double Frame) 1957
My Kingdom for a Hearse 1957
The April Robin Murders 1958
    (completed by Ed McBain)
But the Doctor Died 1967

Craig Rice Collected Short Stories

The Name is Malone 1960
The Murder of Mr. Malone
The Tears of Evil
His Heart Could Break (AKA Hanged him in the morning)
Good-Bye Forever
And the Birds Still Sing
He Never Went Home
Life Can be Horrible
Good-Bye, Good-Bye
The Bad Luck Murders (AKA Dead Men's Shoes)
The End of Fear
The People Vs. Withers and Malone 1963
    (with Stuart Palmer)
Once Upon a Train
Cherchez la Frame
Autopsy and Eva
Rift in The Loot
People vs. Withers and Malone (AKA Withers and Malone, Crime-Busters)
Withers and Malone, Brainstormers

Craig Rice Uncollected Short Stories

(stories not published in **The Name is Malone** or **The People vs Withers and Malone**)

Dead Men's Shoes (<u>Baffling Detective</u>, July 1943)

The Velvet Tigress (<u>Saturday Home Magazine</u>, 1946)

The Rich Die Too (<u>Saturday Home Magazine</u>, 1946)

Death in the Moonlight (<u>Popular Detective</u>, March 1953)

Don't Go Near Him (<u>Manhunt</u>, May 1953)

Dual Personality

Hanged Him in the Mornin' (<u>Verdict</u>, June 1953)

A Quiet Day in the County Jail (<u>Manhunt</u>, July 1953; **The Best From Manhunt**, Perma Books, 1958; **The Bloodhound Anthology, Boardman**, 1959; Cream of the Crime, Holt, 1962; Harrap, 1964)

The Dead Mr. Duck (<u>Verdict</u>, Aug 1953; <u>EQMM</u>, Jan 1959, as The Man Who Swallowed a Horse; **Ellery Queen's 1966 Anthology**, Davis, 1965; **Ellery Queen's Minimysteries**, World, 1969; **101 Mystery Stories**, Avenel, 1986)

Motive (<u>Verdict</u>, Sept. 1953; <u>EQMM</u>, Aug. 1959 as Smoke Rings)

The Bells are Ringing (Manhunt, Nov. 1953)

Murder Marches On (Manhunt, Dec. 1953; <u>Manhunt</u>, Apr./May 1967, as The Dead Undertaker)

The Last Man Alive (1953; **My Best Murder Story**, Merlini 1955, Boardman, 1957)

... And Be Merry (<u>Manhunt</u>, Jan. 1954)

I'm a Stranger Here Myself (<u>Manhunt</u>, Feb. 1954; <u>Manhunt</u>, July, 1965 as Alias:Trouble)

The Little Knife that Wasn't There (<u>Malcolm's</u> May, 1954 <u>EQMM</u>, Aug., 1961 as Malone and the Missing Weapon)

I'll See You in My Dreams (<u>Nero Wolfe Mystery Magazine</u> June 1954)

No Vacancies (<u>Manhunt</u>, June 1954)

Murder in the Family (Saint, Nov. 1954/ March 1955; **Saint Mystery Library No. 6**, Great American 1959)

Flowers to the Fair (Manhunt, 25 Dec. 1954; Manhunt, Aug - Sept 1966 as A Weakness for Women)

Beyond the Shadow of a Dream (<u>EQMM</u>, Feb. 1955; **Best Detective Stories of the Year 1956**, Dutton 1956 / **Best American Detective Stories of** the Year 1956, Boardman 1956)

Mrs. Schultz is Dead (<u>Saint</u>, March 1955 / Aug. 1955)

No Motive for Murder (<u>Saint</u>, July 1955 (US)) (nv) (premise for Knocked for a Loop)

Shot in the Dark (<u>Manhunt</u>, Aug. 1955) (nv)

The Headless Hatbox (<u>Double-Action Detective 3</u>, 1955) (nv) (premise for My Kingdom for a Hearse)

Breaking Point (<u>Detective Files 103</u>, 1956) (tc)

The Campfire Corpse (<u>Detective Files 103</u>, 1956) (tc)

Death in a Pick-up Truck (<u>Detective Files 103</u>, 1956) (tc)

Do Not Disturb (<u>Detective Files 103</u>, 1956) (tc)

Frankie and Johnnie, M.D. (<u>Detective Files 103</u>, 1956) (tc)

House for Rent (<u>Detective Files 103</u>, 1956) (tc)

Identity Unknown (<u>Detective Files 103</u>, 1956) (tc)

No Motive (<u>Detective Files 103</u>, 1956) (tc)

No One Answers (<u>Detective Files 103</u>, 1956) (tc)

One Last Ride (<u>Detective Files 103</u>, 1956) (tc)

The Perfect Couple (<u>Detective Files 103</u>, 1956) (tc)

Small Footprints (<u>Detective Files 103</u>, 1956) (tc)

The TV Killer (<u>Detective Files 103</u>, 1956) (tc)

The Woman Hater (<u>Detective Files 103</u>, 1956) (tc)

The Frightened Millionaire (<u>Saint</u>, April 1956 / Aug. 1956; **Saint Mystery Library No 4**, Great American 1959; **Academy Mystery Novellas: Women Write Murder**, Academy Chicago, 1987) (nv)

Dead Men Spend No Cash (<u>Suspect</u>, Aug. 1956)

The Quiet Life (<u>Mike Shayne Mystery Magazine</u>, Sept. 1956)

The Deadly Deceiver (<u>Pursuit</u>, Nov. 1956)

No, Not Like Yesterday (<u>Saint</u>, Nov. 1956 / Dec. 1957; **Best Detective Stories of the Year 12**, Dutton 1957 / **Best American Detective Stories of the Year 8**, Boardman 1958)

Say It With Flowers (<u>Manhunt</u>, Sept. 1957; **Best Detective Stories of the Year 13**, Dutton 1958; **Best American Detective Stories of the Year 9**, Boardman 1959)

Cheese It, The Corpse (<u>Manhunt</u>, Nov. 1957)

One More Clue (<u>Manhunt</u>, April 1958; **Best Detective Stories of the Year 14**, Dutton 1959 / **Best American Detective Stories of the Year 10**, Boardman 1960; Perfect Crimes, St. Martin's, 1989)

The Very Groovy Corpse (<u>Saint</u>, Nov. 1958 / June 1959; **Saint Mystery Library No. 1**, Great American, 1959)

They're Trying to Kill Me (<u>Saint</u>, Feb. 1959 / Dec. 1959)

Wry Highball (<u>EQMM</u>, Mar. 1959; **Ellery Queen's Choice 14**, Random House 1959, Crime Club 1961)

Hard Sell (Ed McBain Mystery Magazine 1, 1960; **Best Detective Stories of the Year 17**, Dutton 1962 / **Best American Detective Stories of the Year 12**, Boardman 1963; **Crime Squad**, NEL, 1968; **AHP: A Month of Mystery**, Random House, 1969; **AHP: Terror Time**. Dell, 1972)

The Butler Who Didn't Do It (AHMM, June 1960; AHP: **16 Skeletons from My Closet**, Dell, 1963)

How Now, Ophelia (EQMM, June 1947 as Michael Venning)

** (tc) = true crime story

 (nv) = novella

Craig Rice films

Danger Signal. Warner Brothers. 1945. Faye Emerson, Zachary Scott, Dick Erdman, Rosemary DeCamp. Directed by Robert Florey. Uncredited screenwriting by Craig Rice.

The Falcon's Brother. RKO, 1942. George Sanders, Tom Conway, Jane Randolph, Don Barclay, Amanda Varela, George Lewis. Directed by Stanley Logan. Written by Craig Rice and Stuart Palmer.

Falcon in Danger. RKO. 1943. Tom Conway, Jean Brooks, Elaine Shephard, Amelita Ward, Cliff Clark. Directed by William Clemens. Written by Fred Niblo, Jr. and Craig Rice.

Having Wonderful Crime. RKO, 1945. Pat O'Brien (Malone), George Murphy (Jake Justus), Carole Landis (Helene), Leonore Aubert, George Zucco. Directed by Eddie Sutherland. Available on video.

Home Sweet Homicide. 20th Century Fox, 1946. Randolph Scott, Lynn Bari, James Gleason, Peggy Ann Garner, Connie Marshall, Dean Stockwell. Directed by Lloyd Bacon. Based on the novel of the same name. Craig also wrote the screenplay.

The Lucky Stiff. United Artists, 1949. Brian Donlevy (Malone), Dorothy Lamour, Claire Trevor, Irene Hervey, Robert Armstrong. Directed by Lewis R. Foster. (No Justuses).

Mrs. O'Malley and Mr. Malone. MGM, 1950. James Whitmore (Malone), Marjorie Main (Withers-O'Malley), Ann Dvorak, Don Porter, Dorothy Malone. Directed by Norman Taurog.Loosely based on one of the Withers-Malone stories.

The Underworld Story. United Artists, 1950. Dan Duryea, Herbert Marshall, Gale Storm, Gary Moore, Howard de Silva. Directed by Cyril Endfield. Originally called The Whipped and based on a Craig story.

The Eddie Cantor Story. Warner Brothers, 1953. Keefe Brasselle, Marilyn Erskine, Aline MacMahon, Arthur Franz, Will Rogers, Jr.. Directed by Alfred E. Green.

Lady of Burlesque. UA, 1943. Barbara Stanwyck (Dixie), Michael O'Shea (Biff), Janis Carter, Pinky Lee. Directed by William Wellman. Produced by Hunt Stromberg. Craig's agent called this film a mess (originally titled Queen of Burlesque) and she didn't receive screen credit for it. Based on The G-String Murders and fueled speculation about the authorship of the novel.

INDEX

Who Was That Lady?